PERSONHOOD ANI

PERSONHOOD AND PRESENCE

SELF AS A RESOURCE FOR
SPIRITUAL AND PASTORAL CARE

EWAN KELLY

t&tclark

LONDON • NEW YORK • OXFORD • NEW DELHI • SYDNEY

T&T CLARK
Bloomsbury Publishing Plc
50 Bedford Square, London, WC1B 3DP, UK
1385 Broadway, New York, NY 10018, USA

BLOOMSBURY, T&T CLARK and the T&T Clark logo are
trademarks of Bloomsbury Publishing Plc

First published in Great Britain 2012
Reprinted by Bloomsbury Academic 2013, 2015, 2017, 2018

A catalogue record for this book is available from the British Library.

A catalog record for this book is available from the Library of Congress.

ISBN: HB: 978-0-567-61741-5
PB: 978-0-567-28328-3

Typeset by Newgen Imaging Systems Pvt Ltd., Chennai, India
Printed and bound in Great Britain

To find out more about our authors and books visit
www.bloomsbury.com and sign up for our newsletters.

For Stuart, Alasdair and Fraser

Contents

Acknowledgements

I would like to acknowledge, with thanks, the following works:

Sydney Carter, reproduced by permission of Stainer & Bell Ltd, London, England from 'Mother Teresa'.

Raymond Carver, extract from 'Late Fragment' from All of Us: The Collected Poems (The Harvill Press, 1996)

Thomas A. Clark extracts from The Hundred Thousand Places (Carcanet Press, 2009)

Ruth Burgess, 'Risk-Taking' from Wrestling and Wrestling: Exploring Stories of Spirituality from Britain and Ireland, edited by R. Harvey (Churches Together in in Britain and Ireland, 1999)

Kathy Galloway, 'Desert 1' from Talking to the Bones (SPCK, 1996) by permission of SPCK.

Allen Ginsberg, 'These knowing age' from Death and Fame: Poems 1993-1997 (Penguin Books, 1999) by permission of the Wylie Agency (UK) Ltd

Andrew Greig, 'Down by the Riverside' from This Life, This Life: Selected Poems 1970-2006 (Bloodaxe Books, 2006)

Michael Hare-Duke, Extracts from Playtime from Hearing the Stranger (Cairns Publications, 1994). www.cotter.cairns.co.uk

Stanley Kunitz, 'Touch Me' from Passing Through: The Later Poems New and Selected. Copyright 1995 by Stanley Kunitz. Used by permission of W.W. Norton & Company, Inc.

Ann Lewin, 'Disclosure' is taken from Watching for the Kingfisher and is copyright Ann Lewin and Canterbury Press. Reproduced with permission.

Acknowledgements

Norman MacCaig, extract from 'A corner of the road, early morning' from The Poems of Norman MacCaig (Polygon, 2009)Michael Malone 'In the Raw' from Running Threads, poems by J. Hughes, R. Love, M. Malone and S. Templeton. (Makar Press, 2006)

Sonya Rose, 'Eighth Day' from Poems in the Waiting Room, with permission.

Andrew Rudd, 'Dwelling' with permission (www.freespace. virgin.net/sound.houses/)

R.S. Thomas 'Kneeling' and 'St Julian and the Leper' from Selected Poems 1946-1968 (Bloodaxe Books, 1986)

R>S. Thomas, 'Groping' from Collected Poems, 1945-1990 (Phoenix Giants, 1993). Permission by The Orion Publishing Group,

William Stafford, 'The Little Ways that Encourage Good Fortune' from The Way It Is: New and Selected Poems. Copyright 1973, 1998 by William Stafford and the Estate of William Stafford. Reprinted with permission of the Permissions Company, Inc. on behalf of Graywolf Press, Minneapolis, Minnesota, www.graywolfpress.org.

Brian Wren, reproduced by permission of Stainer & Bell Ltd, London, England from 'Great God Your Love Has Called Us Here'.

Thanks to David Lyall and Neil Pembroke for their constructive feedback and encouragement after reading a previous draft, and to Sam Wells for his support and guidance.

1

Introduction

The compassionate provision of pastoral or spiritual care does not begin with an assessment of another's needs. On the contrary, it begins with an awareness of who we are as carers and what we bring to a particular encounter. What is the interpretative framework through which we process and filter our experience of another? What are the different aspects of our human makeup that shape the manner in which we relate with others, the world around us and, thus, ultimately with God?

> you will need to know
> who you are, to walk
> by the solemn lochs
>
> you will have to take on
> the volume of a cloud
> to move with circumspection
>
> you will need to wear
> boots of lead, to walk
> by the solemn lochs

In order to interact meaningfully as a walker with the 'solemn lochs'[1] described in Thomas Clark's (2009, 90) poem of a Scottish landscape, *The Hundred Thousand Places*, with other people or, indeed, with God, we first need to know something of ourselves. The reality of our experience in any context and at any particular time is unique. It is never the same as another's; it is subjective and never objective. More than that, it is

---

1 *Loch* is the Scots word for lake.

of the moment; our experience will not be the same as it was in the past nor in the future. It is socially constructed with the other we are relating to and is shaped by the surroundings or circumstances we are in. North American pastoral theologian Nancy Ramsay puts it this way: 'Relationality clearly points to ways knowledge is inevitably social and therefore perspectival and relative' (2004, 166). How much of the solemnity felt by being next to the loch is the loch itself or the weather, the surrounding context or is it what is already within me at that time? In order to discern something of the reality of another person's mood (as well as a loch's) and their perceptions, meanings or questions, we need to be aware to some extent of our own. Otherwise, the encounter may become more about our realities rather than a co-construction of both theirs and ours. We might like to think we can be purely objective in our judgements but what we construct as our interpretation of an interaction is just that – our understanding of the encounter experienced and processed through our subjective lens. In order then to seek a closer or more nuanced interpretation of the living text we are interacting with, we need to have some understanding of the prescription of our lens: our text, our story informed by our experience and familial and cultural conditioning.

In his book, *Ways of Seeing*, about engaging with art, John Berger helps underline the dynamic relationship between what or who is being interpreted and the interpreter:

> The way we see things is affected by what we know or what we believe. In the Middle Ages when men believed in the physical existence of Hell the sight of fire must have meant something different from what it means today . . . We never look at just one thing; we are always looking at the relation between things and ourselves. Our vision is continually active, continually moving, continually holding things in a circle around itself, constituting what is present to us as we are. (1972, 1)

Unless we are aware, to some degree, of what and who we are, how much of the other are we really going to see, hear, feel or understand? Moreover, not only do we need to be cognizant of our inner landscape, we need to be reasonably comfortable with it as we seek to create a safe space with, and for, patients and parishioners to be themselves in. The Dutch pastor and spiritual guide Henri Nouwen reflects:

> What does hospitality as healing power require? It requires first of all that the host feel at home in his own house, and secondly that he create a free and fearless place for the unexpected visitor. (1979, 89)

Personhood and Identity

As the different facets of our humanity are explored in this text, personhood will be utilized as the overarching term to which these aspects of our make-up belong. For Vernon White, *personhood* is 'a continuous "substratum" or "thread" of being which persists throughout all human lives and distinguishes them from all other creatures' (2002, 45). Personhood does not equate with the notion of a soul, rationality, a person's conscience or moral sensitivity, but it may relate to all of these. White, however, does insist that it is:

> something intrinsically relational: our personhood exists by its relation to other persons, divine and human. However, that does not mean it is reducible to mere 'relation'; there must be some unique centre with which to relate to others which is not just the 'relation' itself. (2002, 45)

Our personhood is the relational aspect of our *identity*. White refers to identity 'as an inclusive term covering all significant and distinctive aspects of human being' (2002, 44). Our identities are that with which we are left when we are stripped bare. Identity is what defines each one of us as unique human beings and is the embodiment of our sense of self. Our identities relate to that which grounds us, formatively shapes us and provides a basis for our living, decision-making and relating. Therefore, identity is linked with story – our personal stories and the communal ones which inform it. Roberts builds on this:

> Identity is not snatched out of the void. It has roots, reasons and history. We talk a lot about story but without the heard-headed recognition that story is determinative. It makes us – individuals and society – who we are: that is, history matters. Identity has threads that require both recognition and the capacity to hold onto them. (2007, 152)

Personhood involves the different relational aspects or dimensions of our human makeup through which our identities impact on us, on others and on our relationship with God. For example, in growing up, my identity as a young Scots Presbyterian male may be have been revealed, stereotypically, in relationship with others through a reticence to express my emotions verbally, a dislike of involvement in public physical displays of affection and a strong work ethic. These aspects of my developing personhood were how others and I experienced the living out of my adolescent identity.

Defining the terms *personhood* and *identity* is not a straightforward task; both are complex and elusive to describe. Scholars from a variety of academic disciplines have attempted to do so – including sociologists, philosophers and psychologists. My brief descriptions are far from complete. However, they offer an adequate basis from which to enable the exploration of different aspects of our human personhood from a pastoral theological perspective.

Aims of the Book

The purpose of this book is to offer an aid to those who seek to understand their individual personhood better, with a view to enhancing the quality of the pastoral relationships they are in and will enter into. Here the reference point for reflexivity is the caring relationship, but as we are fundamentally the same beings in personal and professional relationships, then perhaps readers may also find themselves reflecting on what they bring to a variety of relationships, including that of theirs with the sacred. The longer I am involved in forming relationships with others who are seeking to make sense of their lives and discover or rediscover that which gives meaning and purpose to their living in the present, the more I believe in two fundamental principles.

First, the greatest asset which any of us offers to another in caring relationships is ourselves, or to be more precise, our reflexive selves – the self which we have reflected upon. In the fullness of our humanity, including all our vulnerabilities and wounds, we have the capacity to create grace-filled relationships with others who seek our care. Our ability to do so is greatly enhanced the more self-aware we are. Nouwen was also convinced that to give of self in caring relationships required not only possessing resources to offer but an awareness of what those resources were:

> self affirmation and self-emptying are not opposites because no man can give away what he does not have. No one can give himself in love when he is not aware of himself. Nobody can come to intimacy without having found his identity. (1978, 51–2)

Such awareness does not happen easily nor without intention or experience to reflect on and time in which to do so. We need to give ourselves permission to regularly take that time and space in which to reflect alone or with the support and affirmation of a trusted and gifted other(s). Such ongoing reflexivity can be arduous and painful at times, as well as creative and rewarding. It is the stuff of formation and reformation, shaping not just who we are but, more importantly, who we perceive we are.

This book was written after many years of offering pastoral and spiritual care in parish, hospital, academic and hospice settings. It came to fruition after much ongoing reflection on my professional practice and personal life, which includes a whole range of human experiences from fulfilment in loving relationships to significant losses and bereavements. More than 25 years ago, an American Lutheran pastoral theologian, Gary Harbaugh, wrote at the beginning of his book on the significance of personhood on pastoral practice:

> Pastors are persons. Most of the problems pastors experience in the parish are not caused by the pastor forgetting he or she is a pastor. Most difficulties pastors face in the parish arise when the pastor forgets he or she is a person . . . The pastor is not only a person; he or she is a whole person, a whole person in Christ. (1984, 9)

Harbaugh makes a key point for any spiritual carer in any context; like those we seek to support, we too are human and may also experience the whole range of human thoughts and feelings as we respond to the whole spectrum of experiences in our lives that any human may have to live through or with. We are special and unique in the eyes of God, first and foremost because we are women and men made in the image of God, not because we believe we have a vocation to care for others in God's name. We are not immune to the struggles and adventures others have because we are professional carers. Harbaugh reminds us that we forget this to the peril of our health and well-being.

The second core principle underpinning the writing of this book is that I believe such purposeful reflection on practice and, thus, deepening self-awareness, is a moral imperative for those entrusted with the care of souls. Not to do so is at best to offer others second-rate care and, at worst, encounters can become contexts where we work through our own unresolved issues rather than supporting others as they seek a safe space in which to explore theirs. Stephen Muse, an American counsellor trainer, puts it this way:

> the problem is not so much that persons entering ministry are wounded, but that they do not know or attempt to avoid knowing the extent of the injury and how it can affect them in ministry. (2000, 259)

If we do not have a degree of self-awareness of what we bring or carry into a caring encounter, we not only put our health in danger, but potentially the well-being of those we seek to care for. Self-awareness is not only necessary to maintain our humanity and integrity in ministry but is an ethical requirement to safeguard the emotional and spiritual lives of those we work with. We are storied people and we bring our story, including our beliefs, questions, worldviews, experiences (both reflected upon or not), prejudices, assumptions, and family and personal histories into any encounter with another. Smith and Smith helpfully put it this way:

> It is all too easy when listening to some story or issue to transfer our own meanings and emotions onto it, rather than allowing the truth to surface . . . If people are not in touch with who they are and what they think important then it is difficult to see how they can know another (Palmer 1998). Their sense and appreciation of others and the issues they face will be clouded and cluttered with debris. (2008, 20)

Potentially, any part of our personhood may be consciously or unconsciously touched, challenged or transformed by our experience of offering care. How we deal with this in the present moment and afterwards will not only inform our professional relationships in the present, but future and personal ones too. Being self-aware about the different dimensions of our personhood and intentionally seeking to develop strategies and relationships where these can be explored and our experiences reflected upon, are important not only to remembering we are persons. Such discernment, reflection and activity are also crucial for best practice and personal thriving (not just surviving!). Conversely, the development of self-awareness through reflection on our personal relationships also informs our knowledge of the aspects of self and how we may deal with those different dimensions, likeable or not, in any relationship. Andrew Greig, a Scottish author and poet whose work is informed by his own practice of meditation and mindfulness, in his novel *Electric Brae* explores the opportunities for a deeper understanding of self within the context of intimate relationships, including ones which painfully fail. Jimmy, Greig's main character, a rock climbing oil rig roughneck and divorcee, addresses his former lover Ruth at the end of their turbulent relationship:

> 'In the end,' he concluded, 'for what it's worth I now think we have to carry who we are and not dump it on ships or mountains or sunsets or having babies or anything else.'
>
> 'Hmm,' she said. 'That sounds hard.' (1997, 237)

As Ruth succinctly states, it is challenging to learn how to carry who we are and realize there is potential for discarding unwanted and uncomfortable debris onto other people, relationships and situations. However, we do not have to tackle this steep learning curve on our own.

Over the years I have been indebted to many people, including colleagues, friends, family members, supervisors, mentors, spiritual directors and therapists who have helped me to understand better who I am and how I relate, both to others and the Other. As it is for all of us who partake in this ongoing, risky and sometimes painful venture, as human beings and caring professionals, there are always potential possibilities for growth and learning. It is a never-ending journey of discovery during which we will undoubtedly continue to project our detritus onto others, as they will with us. Hopefully, however, we will become more aware of the complexity of the dance we dance in our human relationships in the process.

In the introduction of a book, it is often also helpful to dispel any assumptions about what the text may be about. This is not a book about personality, character or temperament typing, helpful though the use of tools such as Myers Briggs Type Indicators or the Enneagram may be in developing self-awareness.[2] Nor does the text contain, in the main, a treatize about utilizing a variety of psychotherapeutic approaches to promote self-understanding, though concepts such as counter transference from the psychodynamic school of thought, will be discussed as aids to self-understanding. Instead, this book originates from reflection on practice and the experience of sharing in caring relationships. In doing so, an increasing awareness has arisen of the variety of human facets which may enhance or limit our ability to be present with others and relate attentively.

These dimensions of our personhood are primarily explored through a theological lens, as this is what makes the role of the spiritual or pastoral carer, who is rooted in the Christian tradition, distinctive.

Utilizing Poetry

In becoming one with itself my spirit is one with the world.

The dull aching tension is gone, all hostility and dread.
(MacDiarmid, 1935, 169)

---

2   As Gary Harbaugh (1984) helpfully underlines, such personality indicators give general guidance in relation to personality traits and associated ways of working or relating to others and self. Myers-Briggs Types Indicators, for instance, are not intended to describe the unique personhood of an individual or to outline prescriptively their normal patterns of relating.

In seeking to explore the different facets of what it is to be human living in dynamic relationship with self, others, the natural world and God, over the years I have found, like countless others, the paucity of language in poetry far more descriptive and eloquent than my copious prose (others find music likewise but this is not so helpful on the printed page!). I have, therefore, utilized poems not only as a means of making or underlining a particular point or argument but intentionally to help you, the reader, engage in reflection about your personhood and its impact on practice.

Part I
Gifted Self

2

The Beloved Self

'I never found a man that knew how to love himself.'
Othello, Act 1, Scene 3

Shakespeare, ever the perceptive commentator on the human condition, gets to the source of our frequently subconscious and, thus often unarticulated, unease with life and relationships – our lack of love for ourselves. This chapter seeks to explore the significance the implications of self-love, or rather lack of it, on the spiritual and pastoral care we seek to offer within a theological framework. In doing so, we get to the heart of what holds us and sustains us in our provision of care for another.

> And did you get what
> you wanted from this life, even so?
> I did.
> And what did you want?
> To call myself beloved, to feel myself
> beloved on the earth.

Raymond Carver (1996, 294 cited by Spence 1998, 266) in his poem *Late Fragment* expresses that which fundamentally each of us seeks in life, the joy and security of feeling beloved. Carver's poem serves as a reminder of the crucial issue which is at the heart of pastoral theology and will be explored in this chapter. To what extent do we, as pastoral and spiritual carers, believe we are beloved of God – unconditionally loved as we are, for who we are, irrespective of our failures and foibles and our triumphs and trials?

As human beings, we all desire to find a meaningful, purposeful place for ourselves in our families, in our communities (those in which we live and work) and, ultimately, in the world, in relation to others and to God. We all want to feel needed, appreciated and affirmed in our roles and our relationships. In the field of pastoral and spiritual care, however, there is potential for us to immerse ourselves in the care and concern of others, seeking to gain our worth through affirmation from others and striving to achieve status and community recognition. We can develop patterns of ministry and ways of working that are unsustainable and potentially harmful for self and others. If our identity and our feelings of self-worth are solely equated with our pastoral activity or reputation, then we will sooner rather than later enter a spiritual, psychological and physical 'desolate pit';[1] a 'miry bog'[2] from which we will not emerge without considerable support and carrying slow-healing wounds. Such experiences are potentially life changing, even life enhancing, when they are reflected upon theologically and inform not only future practice but self-understanding. However, the realization and belief that God loves not for what we do but who we are, warts and all, can prevent, or at least counter, such self-destructive drivers. Some of us will not manage to begin to seek embracing such a theological perspective till we have become drained of our all resources in the darkness of the quagmire created by our own harmful behaviour. For others, such an internal tension may remain with us, consciously or unconsciously all our days, being revisited and, hopefully, reclaimed through support and supervision, without necessarily reaching crisis.

In his perceptive book *Waiting on God*, Scottish Redemptorist priest Denis McBride meditates on the significance of a short exert from Luke's Gospel which relays Jesus's response to the exuberance of the 70 basking in the success of their mission,

---

1   Psalm 40: 2.
2   Ibid.

'Nevertheless, do not rejoice at this, that the spirits submit to you, but rejoice that your names are written in heaven'.[3]

> Jesus leads them away from the immediacy of the pres-
> ent – in this case a successful mission, but that could
> easily change with circumstances – to focus on the ulti-
> mate ground of their identity, one that has nothing to do
> with success or failure: the everlasting truth that they are
> loved and cherished by God. In the language of Tillich,
> this is 'the courage of our confidence' that is not built on
> ourselves or on our performance but is founded in the
> belief that God loves and accepts us. (2003, 182)

As Jesus is baptised in the Jordan by his cousin John, 'a voice came from heaven, "You are my beloved Son; with you I am well pleased."'[4] If we are able to hear and own these words for ourselves and understand that God loves as a beloved son or daughter with whom he is well pleased unconditionally, this potentially liberates us from having to build and main-tain our self-esteem through action and seeking affirmation from those we care for. Such a belief that we are loved by God for who we are rather than for what we do enables us to risk reaching out to others in love. It frees us from the tyranny of fear, feeling we have to be sure we will get things 'right', improve another's lot in life or make a difference to be lovable. If in caring relationships the offering of ourselves through a visit, our touch or verbal response is mistimed or unwanted, we may be perturbed by any upset caused to the other and the sense of rejection we may inwardly feel. However, appreciat-ing for ourselves that not only are we human and fallible and bound to make mistakes from time to time but, like those we seek to care for, we too are beloved of God, enables us after some learning through reflection on our practice to risk

---

3 Luke 10: 17–20 – verse 20 quoted here.
4 Mark 1: 11.

again. Ruth Burgess, in her poem *Risk-Taking*, describes God as a risk-taker who created us out of love. God risks, we risk and when we grow through such risk-taking, God shares and rejoices in that, too.

> You are a risk-taker God
> an experimental potter
> a wild artist
> a sculptor of passion
> an adventurer
> a poet of justice and truth.
>
> Yours is an ongoing creation
> growing, changing, dancing,
> a story that is shaped
> in the telling,
> a life that is pregnant
> with joy and with pain.
> And you made us,
> in your energy, in your image,
> holy and loving and courageous;
> needing to risk the
> power of beginning
> and to grow. (1999, 114)

We are empowered to risk, to make ourselves vulnerable alongside those who are hurting, by God's unconditional love for us. We are held, nurtured and able to grow through learning from our experience because we are beloved. This is the core belief which enables us to risk utilizing and honing our natural caring abilities in creative and collaborative ways, countering restrictive anxieties about failure. It is this theological foundation which sustains and supports us in times of self-doubt and despair.

The professor of pastoral theology at Princeton Theological Seminary, Donald Capps (1993), reflects on the thoughts of fellow countryman Gary Harbaugh (1984) on the risks involved in making choices as part of the ministry of pastoral care. Coming to a lived understanding and acceptance that, unlike the Almighty, he was not omnicompetent, was a turning point in Harbaugh's pastoral work. In discovering that making choices meant he had to rely on the forgiveness and grace of God when he made the wrong decisions was liberating. An understanding of being beloved for who he is, and not for what he did or didn't do, underpinned Harbaugh's epiphany. In the Hebrew Scriptures, a similar message is given to the people of Israel by the prophet Isaiah, who utilizes the metaphor of the depth of passion a bridegroom has for his bride on his wedding day to encapsulate God's feelings for his people: 'as the bridegroom rejoices over the bride, so shall your God rejoice over you'.[5] As a bridegroom delights in his bride without reference to her appearance, abilities or potential achievements, so God delights in us as care givers, without measuring the quality or quantity of our work. There is a sense that God takes great pleasure and joy from God's relationship with God's people in Isaiah's imagery. This theme is reflected on by the central character in Marilyn Robinson's novel *Gilead*. Aware he is nearing his death, Reverend John Ames reflects on his life and beliefs, reminding himself of the pleasure God has in our living, being and performing. Ames, in his old age, has come to an understanding of God's delight in humanity and the sense of parental pleasure God finds in us, God's children.

> Calvin says somewhere that each of us is an actor on a stage and God is the audience. That metaphor has always interested me, because it makes us artists of our behaviour, and the reaction of God to us might be thought of as aesthetic rather than morally judgemental in the ordinary sense . . . I do like Calvin's image, though, because it suggests how God might actually enjoy us.

---

5   Isaiah 62: 5b.

I believe we think about that far too little. It would be a way into understanding essential things, since presumably the world exists for God's enjoyment, not in any simple sense, of course but as you enjoy the *being* of a child even when he is in every way a thorn in your heart. (2005, 141–2)

God not only enjoys us, but God wants us to enjoy being ourselves too. However, for many of us, that can be a struggle. Messages ingrained from early childhood from church and familial cultures can mislead us to believe that we are only lovable through achievement or being someone others want us to be. Loving and serving others, putting their needs before ours, can be a message we absorb in our formative years and that we live out to our detriment. Jesus's teaching is, 'You shall love your neighbour as you love yourself',[6] not 'love your neighbour before or more than yourself'. The implications of owning and living out our sense of being beloved by God in our lives as those whose vocation is to care pastorally and spiritually for others is of great significance. Such a pastoral theology demands of us that we must consider our needs as human beings and as carers as much as we seek to consider those we support. Our attentiveness is not only to the voices of others but to the voices within, and, in doing so, we may hear the voice of the Other in both. Belovedness requires extending the gentleness we seek to offer others to ourselves. It means offering ourselves the kind of self-care that Paul offered the people of Thessalonica: 'But we were gentle among you like a nurse tenderly caring for her own children'.[7]

Rosemary Bailey, in her bibliographical account of the life of her brother Simon, a Church of England priest who lived with, and died from, HIV-AIDS whilst still ministering and being ministered to by his congregation in Yorkshire, wrote

---

6 Mark 12: 31a.
7 I Thessalonians 2: 7b.

about the significance for him of God's gentleness with God's children, including himself. Bailey quotes her brother as he explores what is at the heart of his pastoral theology:

> Priesthood demands that before you announce forgiveness for others you experience it yourself . . . He (Jesus) breathed on them and said, "Receive the Holy Spirit." For centuries the church included in the rite of baptism a continuation of this event. Insufflation it was called – the priest blew into the face of the candidate, blowing out the evil spirit, blowing in the Holy Spirit . . . I thinks it's the very gentleness of this image that has struck me . . . the disciples huddled and hidden away in fear, no doubt hoping for power and courage and strength (rushing winds and flames, perhaps). Instead, Jesus gently blows on them – all the forgiveness of God, all the ministry of reconciliation is in that gentleness. Priesthood is not about power and domination and control. It's about this gentleness, like the breeze in your face on a mountain top, like blowing a butterfly off your sleeve, strong enough to move it, light enough not to hurt it. (1997, 108–9)

In caring for others, it is often easier to be more gentle and forgiving with them than we are with ourselves in our own private and working lives. At a basic level, we have more awareness of our own wrongdoings, potentially harmful thoughts and urges than we do of others. Pastoral and spiritual carers, particularly clergy, who have suffered the emotional and physical consequences of stress tend to be the type of personality who spend much time and energy dealing with internal conflicts and low self-worth (Eadie, 1972). Such personalities are shaped and informed by early relationships in life and reinforced by a theology which feeds a deep-seated need to overcome or quieten inner struggles and promote self-esteem through realizing and then maintaining exceptional standards of behaviour or pastoral practice (even if such a goal is impossible, let alone sustainable). Interpreting 'Be perfect, therefore, as your heavenly Father is perfect'[8] in a literal fashion becomes a stick with which to beat ourselves, inevitably leading to feelings of failure and letting God (or rather the authority figure from early child-hood) down, as none of us will ever be perfect in this life. The cycle of internal dis-ease and low self-regard, fuelled by a theology of perfection (or salvation by works), promotes over-activity and constant striving to be the best one can be, leads to depression, fatigue and lack of fulfilment, and even breakdown.[9] This pattern of destructive behaviour cannot be altered by psychotherapeutic means alone. The issues are not just psychologically deep rooted but are also profoundly spiritual. An alternative theology is required, one which not only sustains and informs healthy living and balanced pasto-ral practice, but also a theology which enables a person and practitioner to be free to risk and, on occasions, to fail, with-out excessive self-remorse.

Georges Bernanos ends his novel *The Diary of a Country Priest* with the central character M. Le Cure reflecting, as he is dying, on his life's pastoral work in a French village:

> How easy it is to hate oneself! True grace is to forget. Yet if pride could die in us, the supreme grace would be to love oneself in all simplicity – as one would love any one of those who themselves have suffered and loved in Christ. (1977, 251)

---

8 Matthew 5: 48. Rather than interpreting the verse as a requirement to develop and maintain a moral character that is without blemish, biblical scholars such as Hill (1987) suggest this verse is a reference to Leviticus 19: 2, 'You shall be holy, for I the Lord your God am holy'. Jesus is, therefore, encouraging his listeners to seek to develop God-centred spiritual lives.

9 Such a theology of perfection which acts as motivation for striving to prove oneself as of worth and lovable through achieving a state of behavioural, moral and spiritual excellence is in direct contrast to a Wesleyan understanding. Wesley believed perfection or holiness to be a gift: something received from God, not constantly worked for.

Le Cure's regret is that he had not discovered this earlier in his life and ministry. Yet, perhaps even if we do understand the importance of the need to love and accept ourselves as beloved children of God and how that frees us to do the same to those we seek to care for, such a theological discovery must be revisited repeatedly throughout a lifetime of reflecting on pastoral practice with trusted others. Our familial or ecclesial enculturation of the idea that love and grace are only for the deserving or have to be earned may be deeply ingrained and, therefore, our ownership of being beloved may meet with much subconscious resistance.

A significant aspect of love within the Judeo-Christian narrative is forgiveness. The story of God's forgiveness for God's children is central to both Old and New Testaments, yet one of the hardest things for any of us as human beings and pastors is to forgive ourselves – to let go of the past, to enable us to concentrate on the present moment. We assure others of such forgiveness and seek to be a non-judgemental, compassionate presence, yet often we carry past words, thoughts and actions which weigh us down and reduce our capacity for caring and fullness of life. The significance of the letting go of burdens that we carry and weigh us down unnecessarily is highlighted in the following tale:

> Two monks were walking along a rather muddy road after a morning's heavy rain. Despite this, they made reasonable progress until they came to what they expected to be a ford, enabling them to easily cross the river in front of them. However, with recent rain, the river was deeper than anticipated and on its bank in front of them was a beautiful young woman.
>
> 'Kind fathers,' she said, 'will you help me cross? The river is swollen and I am afraid if I wade across myself I'll get swept away.'
>
> One monk muttered to his companion that they couldn't help the young woman because it was against their order's

rules to have such contact with a person of the opposite sex, let alone one as beautiful as this. However, without a word in reply, the second monk strode across to the girl, lifted her over his shoulder and carried her safely across the river.

After setting her down on the other side, the two monks continued in silence along their way. A couple of miles later, the first monk spoke again. 'Brother, you really shouldn't have done that, it's against all the guidance laid down by our forefathers.' His friend turned to him and replied, 'My brother, I laid the young maiden down nearly an hour ago . . . you though are still carrying her.'

It is in public worship and in our own private devotions that intentionally we can seek the forgiveness of God, be reminded of our belovedness to God as we are and be restored in our sense of value to God. Worship is potentially both restorative and an ongoing deepening of our theological understanding of what it means to be a beloved child of God. It is an opportunity to lessen our grip on that which we hold onto from the past which prevents us from being the people and pastors God intends us to be. Norman MacCaig puts it this way in his poem *A corner of the road, early morning*:

> By holding tight
> To loosing every hold, I began to see
> What I was not helping myself to be. (2009, 139)

Forgiving ourselves, loosening our hold on past hurts we have inflicted on others and ourselves, is seldom, if ever, a one-off event. It is a process that occurs over time and is the fruit of dealing with painful issues and allowing old wounds to heal (Patton, 2005). Prayer and worship, as with support and supervision, therefore, require to be part of the ongoing regular rhythm of the pastoral and spiritual carer's life.

Just as significantly, worshipping also enables us to practice what we preach; for as those who seek to incarnate *agape* in caring relationships, verbalize God's forgiveness and aspire to embody acceptance, we also need these aspects in our lives for ourselves. Participating in worship offers us opportunities to be formed and reformed by God's story of love and redemption through Jesus Christ as it is spoken and sung, celebrated in water and wine, and heard and interpreted in a local faith community context. Worshipping allows us to receive the affirmation from God that we, too, are loved, cherished and delighted in just as we are. Forrester et al. (1996) offer a reminder that 'Worship is enjoying God'. It is also a time when we recall and enact that God enjoys us too – God's beloved children.

3

Waiting Self

This chapter seeks to examine some of the significant gifts a carer may possess which enables connection with others in times of anxiety or distress, and the development of supportive and potentially transformative relationships. Elsewhere, I have explored the significance of a carer's compassion, charm and discernment in such contexts.[1] Here, I wish to consider the ability to wait with others attentively and be creative, wise, resilient and humorous in such relationships.

There is no doubt that our natural gifts need nurture, honed and cultivated over time with sufficient reflection on their use in practice with colleagues, together with an openness to learning in order to optimize their use and effectiveness. To what extent such attributes are God-given and how much they can be shaped by nurture is an ongoing question. Undoubtedly, some people are more intuitively adept at offering spiritual and pastoral care than others and possess a variety of abilities which they have at their disposal to provide appropriate support to those in need. Moreover, such gifts can be objectively perceived and affirmed by others and, with time, our understanding of what we have been gifted can deepen. Over time, and with reflection, the utilization of these abilities may become more nuanced and creative. In short, however, if we ain't got it we can't solely be taught it.

Discerning our pastoral gifts isn't always straightforward. In our formative years, we are often socially conditioned by our families, education systems and the other communities

---

1   Kelly, E. 2008 *Meaningful Funerals: Meeting the Theological and Pastoral Challenges in a Postmodern Era.* London: Mowbray.

we inhabit to behave in certain ways and aspire to particular goals. In order to please and fit in we commonly do so, even if our natural, and perhaps as of yet, unarticulated, desire is to find meaning in other modes of being and doing. Frequently, it is in mid- or later life with the help of a trusted other(s) that our unease with a particular role or model of relating leads to a deeper exploration of who we are, what gifts we possess and how we might utilize them. Or, we may glimpse, through those layers of learnt patterns of behaviour deep within us, gifts which may be intuited but not yet fully realized. Enabling our natural capabilities to be fully utilized for meaningful care to be given and received may involve a process of ongoing unlearning or letting go of culturally acquired adaptations, with supervision or spiritual direction.

The Ability to Wait Attentively with Another

Kathleen Jamie is a Scottish writer whose observations about attentive waiting being part of a poet's giftedness are pertinent to spiritual and pastoral carers. In a newspaper interview, Jamie says of poetry, 'it's about listening and the art of listening, listening with attention. I don't just mean with the ear; bringing the quality of attention to the world. The writers I like best are those who attend' (Scott, 2005, 21). It is something of this quality of attention, an attuned, non-judgemental presence in our waiting with others, that conveys our concern and our compassion. In such depth of engagement, *agape*, the unconditional love of Christ is to be glimpsed.

In Jamie's collection of short essays entitled *Markings* which reveal her attentiveness to and concern for the natural world and the people around her, she describes her experience of waiting with her husband whilst he was severely ill. Jamie is not a particularly religious person. She is someone for whom the culture and rituals of the institutional church have had little relevance in her adult life, and prayer, as a notion and a need, had been something she struggled with:

> Really I carried it [the question about prayer] around until Phil was so ill, and berated myself for not praying. Could I explain to Phil that – though there was a time, maybe 24 hours, when I genuinely believed his life to be in danger – I had not prayed. But I had noticed, more than noticed, the cobwebs, and the shoaling light, the way the doctor listened, and the tweed fleck of her skirt, and the speckled bird and the sickle-cell man's slim feet. Isn't that a kind of prayer? The care and the maintenance of the web of our noticing, the paying heed? (2005, 109)

Often, in times of distress and anxiety when time seems suspended, our senses can be heightened, but for Jamie, her capacity for attentiveness was not just context specific. What she offered her husband was an attentive, watchful and loving presence in a time of waiting for them both. These were hard yet holy moments where the manner of attending and waiting was reverential and the motivation for doing so love. In Gethsemane, Jesus's disciples failed to offer him such companionship at a time of great uncertainty and fear. Even as her husband was recovering, what Jamie wished for from others was more of the same:

> The nurse who came to scoosh the syringe full of saline and antibiotics into the little faucet in Phil's wrist had done this task so often that she barely needed to look. The antibiotics were already having an effect, killing the bacteria wholesale. She was talking amiably about books, about what Phil was reading . . .

> Attend! I wanted to say to her, though she hardly needed to. Here, I'll do it. I'll kill the infection. I'll do it with attention. Prayerfully, if you like. (2005, 111)

In my early days of working in healthcare chaplaincy, when people asked me what motivated me to take on such a role, at least part of my reply would, half-jokingly, include a reference to a degree of nosiness that I possess in other peoples' lives and stories. I have thought about this often and there is more than a degree of truth in it. In the fields of pastoral and spiritual care, unless we are genuinely curious about and interested in others and their lives, then we are wasting our time and theirs. Curiosity, combined with a sense of reverence in our attending to, such as displayed by Kathleen Jamie, is to see with wonder. Donald Urquhart, a Scots sculptor and artist, has created a piece of sculpture in a wooded setting next to the banks of the river Tay in Perth which encourages those who engage with his artwork in its particular context to do so with awe and reverence. The sculpture is large piece of black marble with the words 'BEHOLD' engraved in large letters in gold leaf on one side. On spotting the large marble stone in the wood, I was drawn to it, curious as to what it was and the reason for its presence. The medium as well as the message encouraged me to look through a different lens not only at the artwork itself but at the trees surrounding it and the river flowing by.

By such 'a quality of looking' (Ryan, 2008, 70), the stories we listen to, and in doing co-construct with others, are sacred. In being with people in times of liminality and transition, in attending and waiting with respect and in expectation, we are on holy ground like our forefather Moses. This future leader of the people of Israel, who paused, turned aside from his daily tasks, looked and listened with curiosity, wonder and a willingness to respond. Moses found the holy in the ordinary, heard God's voice in the mundane, because he was willing to take time, be attentive and risk looking though a different lens.

Entering into the lives and stories of others enables us as listeners not just to encounter the inner world and perceptions of the teller but, potentially, to glimpse something of the mysteries of the Other as well as revealing something of the hidden depths of ourselves. Such discoveries are made not just through reflection on practice with the aid of a pastoral supervisor or spiritual director, but by an attitude and innate gift to be reverently mindful in the moment of what is shared, seen and experienced in the company of another. There is something potentially transcendent and meaning-filled by waiting in such a manner. It not just the act of waiting with others that matters; it is how we wait that is of most significance. W. H. Vanstone, in his counter cultural classic of spiritual writing *The Stature of Waiting*, points to the potential profundity of waiting attentively:

> To man as he waits the world discloses its power of meaning – discloses itself in its heights and its depths, as wonder and terror, as blessing and threat. Man becomes, so to speak, the sharer with God of a secret – the secret of the world's power of meaning. The world is for him no mere succession of images recorded and registered in the brain: it is what Blake saw in his tiger and Kant in the starry heavens – a wonderful terror or a terrifying wonder. Rarely does man rise to such intense receptivity; but even in quite ordinary moments he becomes a point at which something in the world is not only registered but understood, experienced, recognized. Because man is in the world there are points in the world at which things no longer merely exist but are understood, appreciated, welcomed, feared, felt. Man as he waits upon the world becomes a place where the world is received not as it is received by a camera or a tape-recorder but rather with the power of meaning with which it is received by God. (1982, 112)

Waiting in another's uncertainty and experiencing something of their loss of control is paradoxically both to inhabit and hold a liminal space where terrible truths are realized and meaning may be glimpsed or remain elusive. At such times, existential questions are asked and God's presence and purpose frequently doubted. What is not required in response are words of explanation or a theological treatize, but an acknowledgement of pain and more waiting. In such times of limbo and with a lack of sufficient words to express lived experience and our inner response, it is hard to find meaning as a carer let alone as the one who has to endure. And yet, perhaps in waiting attentively with another, there may be a glimpse of something worthwhile and enduringly significant for both. Like Vanstone, the Welsh poet-priest R. S. Thomas points to this in his poem *Kneeling*.

> Moments of great calm,
> Kneeling before an altar
> Of wood in a stone church
> In summer waiting for the God
> To speak; the air a staircase
> For silence; the sun's light
> Ringing me, as though I acted
> A great role. And the audiences
> Still; all that close throng
> Of spirits waiting, as I,
> For the message.
>   Prompt me, God;
> But not yet. When I speak,
> Though it be you who speak
> Through me, something is lost.
> The meaning is in the waiting. (1986, 107)

Such waiting is active and never passive (Nouwen 1996, 359). Andrew Grieg's description of a friend's perceptive approach to fly fishing could easily be a description of the type of waiting involved when being with another in a pastoral relationship: 'It's about the right kind of waiting . . . Attentive, open, neither impatient nor resigned. Just being there, alert, eyes focused yet looking beyond the surface' (2010, 112). This sort of waiting requires considerable concentration and courage and utilizes much spiritual and emotional energy. It requires careful attention not just to what is said but to what remains unspoken, 'and what is expressed in other, more subtle ways' (Leach and Paterson 2010, 34). We need to attend to interpreting the living text before us as well their spoken words. Reverential mindfulness also entails setting aside a quantity as well as quality of time. It means stepping away from tasks and goals and entering into a relationship, a context, where our attention and energy, our very selves, are given over to engaging with expectation for as long as is felt appropriate (by the cared for and carer). Attentive waiting with another is a truly draining and intense activity, simultaneously being present and yet internally active – constantly processing what is heard, seen and felt.

A quality of attention, such as Kathleen Jamie desired for her sick husband and that she herself embodied and described, is far from easy to practice – even if we do possess the innate qualities that enable us to wait with others who are *in extremis*. What is it that prevents us from providing such care at times?

Barriers to Waiting Attentively

On leaving school, I trained and worked as a junior doctor. In the mid- to late 1980s, the model I absorbed was medical and the predominant approach to patient care was task orientated. The main focus of learning was seeking to cure physical ailments, with some heed given to mental health. In engaging with a patient, the aim was to take their medical history, examine them, make some differential diagnoses, and then carry out or organize a series of relevant tests. The role I inhabited was primarily centred on doing to and performing tasks on, and for, patients.

Six years after leaving medicine for divinity school, I found myself back in full-time employment in healthcare, this time as a hospital chaplain in a busy acute teaching hospital. One of the units I visited regularly was neurosurgical intensive care, where critically ill patients were all on life support machines and relatives hung around waiting for signs of recovery or death. For the first few months of working in this critical care unit, I felt extremely uncomfortable – my hands got sweaty, my stomach tightened and my mouth dried up as I pushed open its doors to walk in. With the patience and discernment of my pastoral supervisor, it took me a while to understand my physical reactions and internal responses. In intensive care, I had no task to perform, nothing I could do to make things better or fix the situation for relatives and staff, let alone the patients. No examination to perform, needles or tubes to insert, no tests to organize – I felt de-skilled, helpless and useless. What happened in the unit was out of my control. I perceived I had no significant contribution to make. However, gradually, I became aware that as a chaplain my role was something very different, indeed – it was to wait with people and not to do anything to them. It was to stay with relatives and staff in their state of limbo and not perform tasks on or for them. This was a painful dawning. McBride has something perceptive to say of why this might be:

> In our society there is a direct correlation between status and waiting. The more important your status, the less you have to wait. Waiting reminds us that we are not in charge, that we cannot command instantly whatever it is we have to seek, so we have to wait. (2003, 22)

However, in time, I also discovered that everyone else I encountered, whatever their perceived (by others or self) status in the unit, had a similar struggle and felt helpless to some degree or another. This included doctors, nurses, ancillary staff and relatives. We were all waiting, all in suspense wondering how nature would take its course. All the machines and modern technology were there to support patients, or at least their hearts and lungs, while we waited to see whether their brain trauma (through injury, haemorrhage, tumour or surgery) would settle. This was an epiphanal time for me; my helplessness was a 'touching point' with the helplessness of others who temporarily or more permanently inhabited that liminal space.

In subsequent years, working in hospital, hospice or community settings, the most significant question for me in supporting others at times of loss and transition has become, can I wait with, own and allow to be, my helplessness as well as other peoples? Undoubtedly, the ability to provide others with a 'non-anxious presence' (Newell, 2008) in their time of uncertainty or transition is central to the provision of sensitive pastoral and spiritual care. What is key here is understanding that it is perfectly normal at times to feel helpless or useless in the face of another's situation or personal predicament, and not to feel overly anxious or guilty about having these feelings. In short, it is in normalizing these feelings for ourselves, as well as others, and giving ourselves permission to feel this way that we free ourselves to some degree from being overly uptight and uncomfortable. This can enable us to stay with another when we both sense, as carer and cared for, that, ultimately, the current situation is out of our control and has to be lived through rather than fixed or overcome.

Waiting attentively with another who is suffering or sad, seeking to hold them and the paradoxes and the unanswerable questions both verbalized or sensed in self or the other and allowing all that to be, is an immense challenge for any human being, not just one formerly trained to cure all ills. As humans, we all innately want to make things better for others and ourselves, we want to get rid of pain and regain control; our first inclination is to stick a band aid on any open wound. Experiencing another's pain and loss of control in the face of death, serious illness or loss confronts us with our own fears, anxieties and helplessness. We can be overwhelmed not just by another's spiritual need but also by our need to make a difference, so that we are tempted to intervene too quickly during a pastoral encounter (Leach and Paterson 2010). It can also be our anxiety experienced through the disturbance of the equilibrium of our inner world provoked by waiting with another, that informs our desire to end our attentiveness. Therefore, it is hardly surprising that we find accompanying others at such times so hard and often find ways to cut short or avoid staying with our helplessness. Christy Kenneally tells the autobiographical story of an educative episode in his development as a chaplain whilst a young curate in a hospital in Southern Ireland. He writes honestly about regularly visiting a dying nun and the anxiety and fear this evokes within him:

'How are you, Sister?'
'I'm afraid,' she said simply. I was so shocked that she laughed.
'Well, that makes two of us, Sister. So, what will we do?'
'We'll see,' she said.

She made all the running herself. Some days we talked about something in the news and other days we talked about ourselves, swapping the kind of childhood stories that people place in the foundation of what might become a friendship. Occasionally, I brought her gossip from the streets, stretching chords of contact to the world beyond the walls. As time passed, I grew more comfortable with sitting in her silences, just keeping her company.

'D'ye know,' she said one day, 'you've never offered to pray with me?'
'No,' I said. 'I knew a chaplain once who didn't know what to say. He got more and more uneasy with the silence so he said to the man in the bed, "Will I pray with you?"'

'And what happened?'
'The man said, "Yes, if it helps you, Father."'

She began to laugh until the tears streamed down her cheeks. (1997, 63–4)

We can all find various ways to avoid having to wait with others and to be confronted with their loss of meaning and inner void and in turn our own. By the imposition of our words and actions – offering prayer and ritual to end an uncomfortable visit, filling silence with anxious chatter, making cups of tea or offering to do something to help, we may try to avoid feeling useless. We can even be over quick in offering a hug or a hankie in an attempt to stop tears flowing. Discerning such deflection or avoidance activity and exploring the possible reasons for it with a supervisor or mentor is necessary to sustain and maximize the use of our ability to wait attentively over time.

The Art of Waiting Attentively

Mindfulness within the context of spiritual and pastoral care is allowing a story to be told, to be laid out, to unfold and to unravel, as respect is shown for that unique narrative and its mode of telling. It is to wait with genuine expectation and interest, but more than that, it is to be aware that something more may be encountered in the here and now. Such mindfulness can be practised and heightened; for example, various religious traditions from Buddhism to Christianity contain prayerful exercises or meditation techniques which can enhance a person's ability to be still and be more receptive in any one moment. However, unless a person possesses some natural ability to be reverently mindful, having the gift of being able to look and listen perceptively and be in awe of what is and might be, then any amount of practising spiritual exercises will have limited effect.

Waiting with another, unsure of when and how to intervene, adds to our discomfort. Waiting, seeking to discern when is the right moment to interject or act and whose need would be met by doing so, is an art and not an exact science – there are no formulae or action plans to follow. Making such choices is to risk, and as in all risk-taking, we will sometimes get it wrong. However, this short exert from Thomas Clark's poem *The Hundred Thousand Places* contains sound guidance.

the path turns

don't follow it
wait to feel
the lure of it
(2009, 79)

A sensitive response seeking to meet the perceived spiritual or pastoral needs of another evolves out of waiting with them and being attentive to the shared path already journeyed, the negotiated relationship and the co-constructed story which is shared and shaped by both teller and listener. Judgements, related to the timing and type of intervention to be made, are intuited, lured out of us as a felt response, as much as being cognitively decided. Decision-making as to an appropriate response to another's story is shaped to a greater or lesser degree by natural ability, as well as by reflection on previous experience; it requires practical wisdom.

Waiting with Wisdom

For the Lord gives wisdom; from his mouth come knowledge and understanding.[2]

In the biblical tradition, wisdom is a significant gift from God.[3] After Solomon became king over Israel, he asked for and was given the gift of wisdom rather than power, material

---

2   Proverbs 2: 6.
3   1 Kings 3: 9–12.

wealth or knowledge. For the ancients, wisdom was more than mere intelligence. It also related to morality, integrity, insight and to an awareness of God. Within the field of pastoral care provision, wisdom is closely linked to practical experience. Hunter succinctly defines the two: '*Wisdom* refers to a deep or insightful understanding of life achieved through experience; *practical knowledge* is knowledge about how to do things or how to proceed in certain situations, also achieved through experience' (2005, 1325). The ancient Greeks used the term *phronesis* which combines the quality of depth of insight accrued with the practical application of accumulated knowledge in a particular set of circumstances and at a certain moment in time. In Aristotelian thought, to employ such practical wisdom is to possess a disposition which seeks to act with integrity and for the betterment of others through utilizing a deep understanding of life informed by reflection on experience. Fowler describes *phronesis* as:

> [A] knowing in which skill and understanding cooperate; a knowing in which experience and critical reflection work in concert; a knowing in which the disciplined improvisation, against the backdrop of reflective wisdom, marks the virtuosity of the competent practitioner. (Cited in Willows and Swinton, 2000, 14)

Phronesis is more that just a gift we are given, but requires ongoing reflection on our practice of caring as well as the ability to discerningly refer to that accumulated pool of comparative practical examples which each of us carries with us. It is to creatively utilize such gleaned knowledge in the immediacy of other contexts and caring relationships. As Fowler suggests, such pastoral activity when honed over time appears almost effortless, due to the ability and attentiveness of the carer in the present moment. Cultivating wisdom requires hard work, a high degree of reflexivity and a commitment to engage in reflection on practice with others. It requires risk-taking and learning from times when we don't get it right. This can be hard, as we increasingly live in a risk-averse society in the Western world. We can become so attuned internally to 'avoid doing the wrong thing' that we may suppress our intuition or gut feeling which tells us to risk and act (and, thus, a potentially supportive or healing word or action is blocked).[4]

In ancient biblical tradition, Hannah, after years of infertility, handed her son Samuel over to the care of the temple priest Eli to serve God under his tutelage. From Eli, Samuel learnt about discerning God's voice amidst the internal murmurings of his heart and the interior echoes of authority figures in his early years.[5] In doing so, Eli used his practical wisdom to help hone Samuel's gift for discernment. However, several years earlier, Eli had met a childless and bereft Hannah in the temple.[6] Eli perceived a distressed but drunken woman before him as he saw her lips move in prayer yet heard no words uttered. He quickly jumped to the conclusion that Hannah was drunk without engaging her in conversation and admonished her for being so. It was only after Hannah pleaded her innocence and talked of her inner turmoil that Eli responded with wisdom and a blessing, which helped to salve her wounds.

Eli got it wrong; we will get things wrong, which will affect others and ourselves. However, through possessing some innate common sense, engaging in ongoing intentional reflection on our practice and a willingness to continue to risk, we may, like Eli, utilize *phronesis* to enhance the lives of others and give meaning to our own in doing so.

John Patton, an American pastoral theologian, also reminds us that what he calls 'pastoral wisdom' (2005, 7) is not just about doing the right thing or making the right decisions informed

---

4   The subject of risk-taking is further explored in Chapter 4 in relation to touch in the context of spiritual and pastoral care.

5   1 Samuel 3.

6   2 Samuel 1.

by the wise application of practical knowledge, it is also about being. An aspect of wisdom involves an awareness of who we are and what we may represent for others in different situations and according to their present and previous life experience.

We never know what people carry, what their story has involved and in different moments in their lives what may prevent or prompt them to share themselves with us. In her novel *Gilead*, Marilyn Robinson's main character, John Ames, reflects on a life time of pastoral ministry:

> That's the strangest thing about this life, about being in the ministry. People change the subject when they see you coming. And then sometimes these very same people come into your study and tell you the most remarkable things. There's a lot under the surface of life, everyone knows. A lot of malice and dread and guilt, and so much loneliness, where you wouldn't really expect to find it, either. (2005, 6–7)

Perhaps part of the nurturing of our own pastoral wisdom requires an awareness of the possibility of the burdens our fellow humans bear. Thus, utilizing such a God-given gift requires us to discern the times when others want to share their inner lives and when they don't, to be open to God's promptings and to learn from our experience. To be pastorally wise is also to realize we are not God and that like Eli, we will not always be completely open or sensitive to others' projections and problems. At such times, wisdom is also to hold onto the fact that God wants us to be as gentle with ourselves and our shortcomings as much as we seek to be gentle with others and theirs.

Jean had been diagnosed with a brain tumour – a benign, operable one. The night before her operation, I was called to see her, as she was very anxious and fearful. From our conversation, it was evident that Jean's life had been far from easy. She was a trusting and simple soul whose family had little to do with her and a number of male friends had physically, psychologically and financially taken advantage of her generous and giving nature. Jean had also flitted from church to church, seeking support but she felt she never fitted in. She had clearly picked up from the surgeon's pre-operative discussion that there were possible major complications relating to her impending operation. Jean was naturally very afraid that she might die. She sought reassurance from me that nothing terrible would happen and that God would look after her. Of course, I could not guarantee Jean her safety but after spending time listening to her fears, I sought to normalize her anxiety and offered to end our time together with a prayer. Jean gladly accepted the offer, and together we recognized her natural anxieties and fears and asked God to be with her and the healthcare team involved in her surgery, and to give Jean peace during that night.

Tragically, post-operatively, Jean suffered a massive stoke which rendered her speechless and paralysed down one side. With a heavy heart, I went to visit Jean for the first time after surgery. On seeing me she thrashed the arm which she could still move around against her bedside with all her might and opened her mouth as if to scream but no sound emerged. All I could say was that I was so sorry. Jean's agitation continued and I asked her if she wanted me to leave. At this, she grabbed my hand and wouldn't let go. I remained for what seemed like an age until she finally did. Before I left, I promised to come back the next day if that was what she wanted. It was. For a period of several weeks, whenever I was on duty and in the hospital, I went to spend some time with Jean. Often, I was only there for a few short minutes and at other times she would grab my hand for dear life and keep me waiting with her. Jean could only grunt and most often I felt there was nothing appropriate I could say, yet I perceived Jean needed me to be there and to keep returning during her hospital stay. Countless men she had trusted had abandoned her in the past and the God whom she had sought help from in a time of great fear had done likewise. Yet, paradoxically God hadn't completely given up on Jean because God was embodied in the personhood and presence of the chaplain who waited with her in her distress and, crucially, kept coming back to spend time with her (uncomfortable though it was for the chaplain). Practical wisdom nudged me daily in the direction of Jean's bedspace and informed my mainly silent presence, even when my mouth was sorely tempted to ease my discomfort and helplessness. Eventually, Jean left the acute hospital for further rehabilitation and a chaplaincy colleague took over her pastoral care. As well as a degree of wisdom, such waiting was also informed by faith, even if that faith was repeatedly questioned.

'Waiting is an act of faith that requires risk and holds onto hope. Can we in the face of so much suffering . . . remember God's justice, mercy and love?' (Ackermann 1998, 97, cited by Leach, 2007, 24).

Waiting Creatively

It is only out of waiting with, and our attentiveness to, the lives and stories of others that we can creatively respond to seek to meet their expressed and intuited needs in words or through shared ritual action. Auden affirms the significance of such abilities and the order in which they should be employed:

> The miracle wrought by the Holy Spirit is generally referred to as a gift of tongues: is it not equally a gift of ears? . . . That we may learn first how to listen and then how to translate are the gifts of which we stand most urgently in need and for which we should most fervently pray at this time. (1965, 37, cited by Cotter, 1993, 9)

Betty was a normally active and organized woman in her sixties who was struggling to get her head round the consequences of being told she had advanced cancer that was beyond curative treatment. Ever the pragmatist, Betty pressed the doctor to tell her how long she had to live. Months, possibly just weeks, was the reply. Her head was spinning as practical issues and various family scenarios rapidly came to mind. It was all too much – Betty didn't know how to start getting her head round such bad news and the consequences of it. Betty shared with me something of her confusion and disorientation caused by the enormity of the task facing her and her frustration at not being able to begin to make plans. As I listened and sat with Betty, some words of Desmond Tutu's, spoken in the very different context of post-apartheid South Africa, came to mind – 'The only way to eat an elephant is in small pieces'. At a gut level, it felt right to articulate this to Betty after she'd sighed and sat back exhausted in her chair, evidently finished with telling her story. Quicker than I'd ever imagined, Betty picked up how I was trying to help her reframe her situation. The next day, she phoned her best friend and neighbour to arrange for her come in to the hospital to visit whilst Betty's son would be there. Betty had begun her plan of action; she would begin by telling her friend of her situation – her first small but significant step in regaining some control in her situation.

Waiting attentively and creatively with another is to listen to the telling, and often the retelling, of a person's story. It is to wait and wait some more till we may experience that 'ah-ha moment' (Owen, 2008, 55) in order to respond. This ensures that the response which resonates within us is not forced or contrived, but emerges organically out of our interaction with another where meaningful interpretation may be attempted. At such a moment, we may discern how to intervene or, indeed, whether to intervene at all. Mark Ellen, a journalist, asked the songwriter and poet Leonard Cohen about the creative process involved in songwriting. Cohen replied:

There seems to be a transmission, a moment, and I recognise it. That something somehow leaps out of the meaningless day that one is generally living and it speaks to your heart of some kind of significance. (2007, 86)

We have to seek to be attentive to that moment and to trust our creative abilities as we offer a verbal or an enacted interpretation of the other's story and, where appropriate, utilize the Christian story as an interpretative tool. Seeking to timeously and sensitively facilitate interpretation or reframing of another's experience is to utilize practical wisdom, but again it is also to risk getting it wrong. It is hard waiting for such moments to emerge during an encounter because they sometimes do not come or, rather more often, we fear they will not come. Silence or touch or even tears may be the best response(s) in a certain context and with a particular person, informed by the internal resources we possess at that time.

A couple had found their way to the chaplain's office after being given bad news again in the hospital's assisted reproduction unit; their fourth attempt at assisted conception had failed. Both husband and wife were in their early forties and were emotionally and spiritually drained by the long and tortuous experience of trying and failing to conceive. The process of repeatedly attempting to become pregnant through artificial means was taking its toll on them, as individuals and as a couple. They had mutually come to the decision that if this attempt failed, then they would need to find a way of accepting their infertility and explore other avenues of how they might parent a child. After they had shared their story at some length, I suggested we moved into the hospital chapel next door. There, I laid out four small candles and one larger candle on the communion table and lit them. Husband and wife were then asked to blow out the four smaller candles and then finally, together, the larger one. The couple held hands and did so, but when it came to the last candle there was a significant pause before they glanced at each other and blew. Embracing, husband and wife wept.

Pamela Couture, a feminist pastoral theologian, sums up beautifully the creative dimension of spiritual and pastoral care:

Practical theology reaches into our souls to engage our intellect and our bodies, our being and our doing.

Pastoral care, as one practice of practical theology, draws on the methods and insights of science, but, in the end, is a creative act of imagination. It is an artistic practice which simultaneously engages human gifts, meets human need, and witnesses to a vision of life in which care for persons, for creation, and for God is central. (1998, 27)

Waiting Resiliently

'They [Job's friends] sat with him on the ground for seven days and seven nights, and no one spoke a word to him, for they saw his suffering was very great.'[7]

Being present with another, no matter how distressed they are, for seven days and nights is somewhat extraordinary. However, the extended presence of Job's comforters with him in a time of great adversity does raise the issue of what helps to sustain us as carers when we are faced with great suffering in others and, perhaps, repeatedly over a period of time.[8] Jesus knew how draining it was to meet the needs of the sick, the sad and the outcast. In the story of the short therapeutic relationship he developed with a woman with heavy and prolonged menstrual bleeding, we are told Jesus observed 'power had gone out from me.'[9]

Waiting with others and entering into supportive and potentially transformative relationships requires resilience, a gift which some more than others possess. The concept of resilience is becoming increasingly popular within healthcare. Vanistendal (2003, cited by Monroe and Oliviere, 2006,

---

7 Job 2: 13.

8 Job's sons and daughters had all died suddenly, he had lost all of his herds of sheep and camels, and had developed a terrible skin disease which presented itself in the form of sores all over his body.

9 Luke 8: 46.

22) defines resilience as 'the capacity to do well when faced with difficult circumstances'. Like the other abilities already explored, our natural resilience can grow and be developed over time by learning from living through adversity (Monroe and Oliviere, 2006).

It took courage and perseverance for Christy Kenneally to keep returning to be with a dying nun and perhaps even more to admit he was afraid of doing so. After the nun had laughed at his story of the chaplain who offered prayer to a patient to relieve his own discomfort, Keanneally offered to end their conversation:

> 'Would you like me to leave now?'
>
> 'No, I'd like you to pray with me.'
>
> I'd been saying prayers since I could talk. I was most comfortable with the tried and trusted, and very wary of the scary ones in the ritual that were heavy on guilt, like the small print on a certificate for fire insurance. I had no book now and I was afraid. As a child, I had prayed really hard that my Mam would come back and that Pop and Nan wouldn't die. She didn't and they did. My success rate was poor. But I knew she wasn't asking for an 'asking' prayer. We both knew that she would die, and soon. And so, with great trepidation, I stepped into unscripted waters, simply thanking God for being with us in the stories and the laughs and the silences. And then I was silent.
>
> 'Are you asleep?'
>
> 'No, but I think I can now.'
>
> It was the last time we spoke. (1997, 64)

Accompanying another into the unknown places, the scary places, the dark places of their journey, inwards and outwards, provokes anxiety and fear within us. For, at very least, these experiences remind us of such places in our own lives and living. We need to possess courage and steadfastness to be able to be with others, on a regular basis, who are struggling with uncertainty and transition. For such is at the heart of spiritual and pastoral care; a care which is 'costly and dangerous' (Campbell 1986, 36) and requires us to risk of ourselves, to face what may be uncomfortable for others and for us. This is resonant with God's care for us and our world, in Jesus. Like Jesus, our resilience may also be developed over time through strong supportive social networks, a belief that our efforts make a difference, an ability to reframe challenging situations and through being attentive to our own spiritual lives and relationship with God (with reference also to Monroe and Oliviere, 2006).

The final gift I would like to explore also significantly contributes to our resilience as carers and helps enables us to support others – possessing a sense of humour.

Waiting Lightheartly

We have all experienced the sheer pleasure of being in the company of someone who regularly makes us laugh, whether a friend or a professional performer on stage or on television, someone who has the ability to enable others to 'belly' laugh from the centre of our beings. Relatively few of us have that special talent, but many of us do possess the gift of lightheartness, which contributes to our resilience and ability to cope with life, including our ongoing caring for others. Possessing a sense of humour helps us to:

(1) Live more lightly with ourselves
(2) Deal with the absurdity of the human predicament
(3) Laugh with others as they laugh at their situation

Humour and Living Lightly with Self

Possessing the ability to laugh at ourselves when we perceive our presence, thoughts, words or actions have been less than helpful to another or to ourselves can help us to put things in perspective. A self-deprecating but not self-negating laugh at ourselves can be highly therapeutic. It can also help prevent us taking ourselves and our role or status too seriously. Utilizing such a gift can be transformative and help us to reframe our perceptions (Kohut 1971, cited by Kramp, 2007). Others, of course, can be the stimulus for such laughter.

In the first few months of being employed in a Glasgow hospital as a chaplain, I was invited by an occupational therapist to come and help facilitate an informal conversation about coping with loss with a group of amputees. At the agreed time, I joined the group having coffee in the rehabilitation gym, slightly anxious as to how I would be received and whether patients would want to talk and share their experiences. My occupational therapist colleague asked me to introduce myself and explain what my role in the hospital was. After a couple of minutes of me talking about what I did in general terms, an older man with a broad accent interrupted, 'So yer a sort of minister for the hospital? Do you hold services?' 'Yes, I suppose I am,' I replied, 'and we do have a service on a Sunday morning. Anyone can come. It doesn't matter what fit ye kick with.'[10]

There was a pause and, with a broad grin, the old fellow looked in me straight in the eye and said, 'Well son, that's no much guid to me.'[11] I then looked down to where his legs should have been – he had double above-knee amputations! I wished the ground would open and swallow me up, but everyone else burst out laughing around me. All I could do was to join in. Any tension or sense of people needing to be on their

---

10 *Fit* is Scots for foot. This literally means anyone can come, whether you are Protestant or Roman Catholic.

11 'That's not much good to me.'

best behaviour induced by the minister being around was now well and truly dissolved. The chaplain was certainly human! In many ways, my *faux pas* was the best thing that could have happened – I was warmly received into the group.

Donald Capps describes such humour as 'soul maintenance' as 'it enables us to neutralize or relativize our anxieties about failure' (2005, 113).

Humour and dealing with the absurdity of the human predicament

Utilizing our sense of humour in this manner is not a tool to enable us to hide or escape from the harshness and complexity of life but may help us and others deal with the reality of human experience. In times of great stress, laughter can be very close to tears. How often have we said ourselves or heard others say, 'I don't know whether to laugh or cry'? Commonly, I have heard patients or relatives say with a somewhat ironic smile and a shake of their head that their situation couldn't be the basis for the plot of a soap opera or a popular novel because it's either too complicated or its too horrendous to be believable. They feel the story of their circumstances is so absurd – you couldn't make it up – reality being stranger than fiction.

With reference to Capps (2005), Kramp states humour 'is liberating, since it refuses to suffer the wounds inflicted by reality and yet, at the same time, it does not deny reality; humour is a way of asserting oneself and one's own wishes, in spite of what appear to be tremendous threats' (2007, 630). Lightheartedness is part of what may give us hope in difficult situations and may indeed help foster hope in others (Herthe, 1990).

The ability to laugh with others in their adversity

If we have the ability to laugh with others when they see the humour in the absurdity or complexity of their circumstances, we give them permission to do so and to keep doing so. Many people feel guilty about laughing in the immediacy of death and bereavement. However, having someone with them who is willing to risk enabling them to laugh or to laugh with them can offer release. Visiting families before and after funerals can be a time when tears and laughter often come together. This requires a sense of humour and practical wisdom to gently facilitate and permit such an atmosphere.

Working as a hospice chaplain often meant being with families over a period of time as they waited for their loved one to die. This can be extremely difficult and frustrating for relatives, as often they have to wait far longer than they initially anticipated. How many times do they have to say goodbye? However, one of the lessons I learnt from nursing colleagues fairly early on in palliative care work was that often people die as they have lived. Once a relationship of trust had been developed with a family and the story of the now unconscious patient at least partially heard, a comment that usually brought a response of laughter, a shaking or nodding of heads, a raising of eyebrows and further storytelling was to say something like, 'Bert looks as if he likes the last say', or 'Has Bert always been a stubborn so and so?'

Giving permission to others to laugh in the midst of adversity can lead to storytelling, reframing and re-interpretation. Used with wisdom and discernment, our sense of humour can help deepen peoples' exploration of their story, not just to avoid its reality.

4

Sexual Self

Freud postulated that, as embodied beings, there is an erotic life force within each woman and man which contributes to the totality of the energy and potential for fullness of life that we possess at any point in our lives.[1] How we utilize and direct such primal energy depends on our upbringing, religious and societal influences, and the particular circumstances in which we find ourselves. Such a sexual drive is a core element of our humanity and may stimulate creative and meaningful opportunities to express ourselves as physical, sensual and spirited beings; for example, not just in intimate relationships but in music, dance, art and literature. However, through the ages to the present day, the Church has often negated and decried libidinous energy as something to be suppressed or overcome, rather than acknowledged, celebrated and channelled in fulfilling ways for individuals, families, churches and communities. Stanley Kunitz, in his later years, glimpses the positive influence of his libido whilst gardening, as he writes in his poem *Touch Me*:

> Outdoors all afternoon
> under a gunmetal sky
> staking my garden down,
> I kneeled to the crickets trilling
> underfoot as if about
> to burst from their crusty shells;
> and like a child again

---

1 Freud also proposed that a second primal drive within each of us was destructive or death-seeking – what he termed *thanatos*.

marvelled to hear so clear
and brave a music pour
from such a small machine.
What makes the engine go?
Desire, desire, desire.
The longing for the dance
stirs in the buried life. (1995, 158)

Sexuality is more than the genital expression of an erotic urge; it is something far broader and more complex and mysterious to define. As Kunitz suggests, human sexuality is also about the need for creativity and self-expression (Stewart 1997) as embodied, physical beings.

Historically, the Church, influenced by dualistic Greek philosophy, portrayed the physical (the body) as a lesser dimension of the human makeup in relation to the mind or spirit. However, more contemporary Christian sexual theologizing has reclaimed biblical perspectives, which do not see a tension between the physical and the spiritual. For example:

- being made in the 'image of God' refers to the integration of both these significant aspects of our personhood;
- physical attraction and passionate desire for physical intimacy are intertwined with love and commitment in meaningful sexual relationships[2]
- The Word became flesh and lived among us' reveals a God not only willing to be vulnerable and share our experience but a God incarnate – the Other embodied in human form.[3]

Contemporary sexual theology perceives human sexuality as a gift from God (The House of Bishops of the Church of England, 2003) which 'enables us to be, to become, to love and to enjoy' (Smith, 1990, 20).

---

2   See Song of Songs 7 and 8: 5–7.
3   John 1: 14.

Our sexuality is at the very heart of our identities, how we understand and feel about ourselves (including our bodies) and how and why we relate to others in a variety of ways. American ethicist Stanley Grenz puts it this way:

> Sexuality encompasses our fundamental existence in the world as embodied persons. It includes our way of being in and relating to the world as male and female. Above all, however, sexuality is connected to our incompleteness as embodied creatures, an incompleteness that biological sex symbolizes. Hence, sexuality lies behind the human quest for completeness. This longing for wholeness, which we express through our seemingly innate drive to bond with others, forms an important basis for the inter-personal dimension of existence. (1998, 88)

Our sexuality is part of what stimulates us to reach out and relate to others in personal friendship and within professional caring relationships, as well as to desire erotic pleasure. According to Grenz, there is a deep need for us as human beings to seek connection with and affirmation from others. Sexuality, therefore, is closely entwined with our spirituality and our need for finding fulfilment and purpose in life, especially in and through meaningful relationships.

Sexuality also includes, but is more than, our sexual orientation – 'our affectional orientation towards those of the opposite and/or same sex' (Nelson, 1978, cited by Smith, 1990, 28) – and our sexual identities, behaviours and attitudes which have been socially constructed by familial, ecclesial and societal influences (e.g., increasingly, by the media). Thus, our sexuality is both gift and the product of our current and developmental environments. As the matrix in which we live and move and have our being is continually changing, potentially so, too, is our sexuality and our understanding of it (Heyward 1994). For example, a middle-aged person in a heterosexual marriage may begin to acknowledge hitherto suppressed homo-erotic desires. Such honest ownership of part of a person's sexual identity may be due to intentional inner exploration and the desire for self-actualization, and/or due to increased societal acceptance of the normality of homosexuality. In reality, it may be due to both.

Sexuality, Embodiment and Caring Relationships

'To be born is to be embodied, enfleshed.' Jansen (2004, 36)

'We are rooted in our bodies. At birth, in our play and work together, in our love-making and at our death, it is not simply that we *have* bodies. It is more that we *are* bodies.' (Newell 2000, IX)

How we feel about ourselves as human beings is significantly influenced by our perception of our bodies – what we look like and how attractive or likeable our self-in-body is to others and to ourselves. In our contemporary world, this has never been more so for people of every age. Children, especially girls, are becoming sexualised at an earlier age, encouraged to wear sexually provocative clothing and makeup even prior to puberty, through increasing exposure to targeted social marketing of an unashamedly overt sexual nature. From adolescence to old age, society in the twenty-first century increasingly equates well-being with looking sexually attractive – being slim, firm, well-defined and sensual without wrinkles or grey hair.

Michael Malone's satirical poem *In the Raw* explores the relationship between body image and self-identity.

> Naked toes probing
> the deep pile bedroom carpet,
> I stand braced in honesty
> before the cruel length mirror.

Fine lines that crow
from the side of my eyes
not so difficult to find now.

Testosterone fused hairs bore
through pores on my nose and ears
I turn to appraise the rug
that is my neck, shoulders and back
while skin on my scalp reflects
each available beam of light
with laughing intensity.

Another grey hair sprouts
sternly from my chest
that doesn't quite need a bra
since I started to squeeze out
those press-ups. Mental note –
increase to five a day.

Shit! There's even one
dour hair on my belly.
I contain the relaxed flesh here
with outstretched fingers.
Enough blubber here to feed
a Polar Bear for a month.

The towel drops to snake
around my feet. There's still life
in the flesh hanging here
even if the opportunity for use
is as rare as a cheer in a brothel.

To think the legs that prop me
used to pump around fields of cropped grass
rarely move below a canter
looked quite good in shorts
would not look out of place
behind some chicken wire.

Eyes slowly rise to meet eyes
a man I think I know looks back.
Unanswered questions sulk
in the yolk of his eyes. (2006, 60–1)

Malone, though poking fun at himself, and those of us who relate to his sentiments, is also expressing a sense of loss. A loss which has crept up on him almost unawares and now he wonders who he really is. For Malone is pointing to the intimate relationship between our perception of physical appearance and our identity: fundamentally who we are. This has never been more so than in our contemporary commercial and media-driven world, where status, significance and success in society are proportionate to looks and sexual attractiveness as much as material wealth.

How comfortable do we feel in our own body, especially if our body has changed in recent years in a way which we don't like or want? Do we perceive our appearance and sex appeal measures up to what, for example, the advertising, television and music industries have constructed as desirable, sexy and the cultural norm? How does this affect the way in which we feel about ourselves and the way we relate to others?

Crucially, for pastoral and spiritual carers, reflecting on our sexuality and how our sexuality influences the care that we offer includes thinking and feeling about how we inhabit our own bodies and to what extent we feel comfortable living and relating to others within our own skins. Rowan Williams eloquently states:

Thinking about sexuality in its fullest implications involves thinking about entering into a sense of oneself beyond the customary imagined barrier between the 'inner' and the 'outer', the private and the shared. We are led into the knowledge that our identity is being made in the relations of bodies, not by the private exercise of our will or fantasy: we belong with and to each other, not to our 'private' selves. . . (2002, 8)

Williams stimulates us not only to reflect on the impact of how we feel about our bodies in relationships but also how others relate to our bodies, as well as their self-perceptions and our response to their embodiment. Many patients and parishioners we work with will live with an illness (or the treatment for their illness) or the result of an injury or accident which has significantly changed their body shape. For example, many cancers may cause significant weight loss, or prolonged use of steroids may lead to facial puffiness and substantial weight gain. This will, in turn, impact, to varying degrees, on their sense of self, their self worth and willingness to relate to others. Such significant alterations in body shape may cause a deep-seated self-rejection where, for example, looking in the mirror at their naked self may be too much to bear.

Harry was a 56-year-old widower who had re-married just over three years ago. Following a recent above-knee amputation for circulatory problems, Harry was struggling to adjust. There were the physical challenges of learning to walk again utilizing a prosthesis, especially when the wound on his stump kept breaking down and bleeding. However, other adjustments were proving even more difficult.

Harry had been a big strong athletic man in his youth, who played semi-professional football and, until two years ago when his circulation restricted his ability to exercise, had been a low-handicap golfer. George, the local minister, had become friendly with Harry after he had performed the funeral of Harry's first wife, Betty. George had subsequently married Harry and Wilma and had occasionally played golf with Harry. Wilma was ten years younger than Harry and was an attractive, energetic woman who had become an active member of George's congregation. She phoned George one evening and had asked if he would visit them – she wouldn't explain why on the phone, as she said it was a rather delicate matter.

A couple of days later when George rang the couple's front door bell, Harry answered and before George could get across the doorstep, began to splutter apologies and mutter something about this being all rather embarrassing and stupid. Wilma intervened and invited George into the living room. After making a customary cup of tea, Wilma took the initiative. 'Harry says he wants me to go, to leave. He's taken to sleeping in the spare bedroom and he won't even let me give him a cuddle. What have I done? I love him to bits.' With this she began to cry.

Harry, sitting on the other side of the room, looked increasingly agitated. As Wilma dabbed her eyes, George said, 'Wilma, I don't think Harry's behaviour is to do with how he feels about you.' Then moving his gaze towards Harry, he said, 'It's how Harry feels about himself right now that is causing you both so much pain.'

For Harry, so much of his understanding of self was tied up in his physicality and physical prowess in the past and his now-perceived lack of vigour and manhood in the present. With the loss of his leg, he not only felt physically diminished but he was no longer sure of who he now was. That not only left him feeling bereft, but lost and lacking self worth. A significant aspect of his low self-esteem was a now firmly held view that he was no longer attractive to his wife. Harry's distress was not only sexual, but also deeply spiritual.

Being loved sexually (not necessarily genitally) and loving ourselves as sexual beings is important for human well-being and wholeness. For the pastoral and spiritual carer, such self-love as a beloved, embodied child of God may enable us to be comfortable enough in our own skin to risk utilizing our bodies in a discerning way within caring relationships, to express God's love and compassion significantly through the use of touch.

Sexuality and Touch in Caring Relationships

Skin-to-skin contact has been reported to lower blood pressure, reduce anxiety and stress, and stimulate hormone production (see Uphoff, 2008). Researchers and therapists in both the UK and America, for example Uphoff (2008) and Field (2003), describe such therapeutic benefits of touch leading to the facilitation of bonding and the promotion of well-being and happiness. Attitudes to touch vary according to culture and gender. Field (2003) claims Americans are very non-tactile, except within their family circle and with sexual intimates. She cites the British as likewise, according to the studies of Sidney Jourard (1966) who observed the number of times two people who having coffee together touched. The French and Puerto Ricans, on the other hand, were observed as being highly tactile.[4]

Fisher et al. (1976) in a hospital study found that 85 per cent of patients who were touched (with the purpose of reassuring or comforting them), but only 53 per cent of untouched patients, responded positively about the hospital. They also reported that those who were touched recovered more quickly. In exploring gender attitudes to touch, Fisher and Gallant (1990) found women who were less anxious concerning surgery were touched with the aim of reassuring them than those who weren't. In contrast, men who were touched reported more anxiety. The touched women tended to actively reach out for a nurses' hand and had lower blood pressure in the recovery room, unlike the touched men. Fisher and Gallant (1990) concluded that being touched might make men feel more vulnerable and dependent.

Sutherland (2006) postulates that those who receive little touch in their developing years absorb the message that their bodies are untouchable. As she reflects on this within a psychotherapeutic framework, Andrea Uphoff comments:

> What indeed are we communicating as therapists, contributing to this process, if we withhold physical contact, restrain ourselves from this most basic of all communication? For those who regard themselves as unlovable and undesirable, we fail to provide unconditional positive regard . . . (2008, 212)

---

4 Jourard observed two people sharing coffee in a café in different parts of the world for the same duration. He noted how many times a couple touched. In Paris, they touched 110 times; in San Juan and Puerto Rico, more than 180 times; but in Gainesville, Florida, two people sharing coffee touched twice; and in a café in London, the tally was zero.

The debate within the psychotherapeutic community about the place of touch is more contentious than within pastoral theology.[5] However, within the field of pastoral theology, there is no question about the potential of touch in therapeutic relationships as a potentially healing, affirming and compassionate gesture if we are to follow the example of the embodied life and ministry of Jesus, a ministry in which giving and receiving love and care through touch was central not just to what he enacted but what he taught.[6] In the parable of the Forgiving Father (better known as the parable of the Prodigal Son), we read of the potential of symbolic gesture through touch to convey far more than words often can in situations of complexity and intensity:

> So he set off and went to his father. But while he was still far off, his father saw him and was filled with compassion; he ran and put his arms around him and kissed him.[7]

An errant son who has abused his father's trust is hugged and kissed by a father who runs to greet him – all that Jesus seeks to communicate to his listeners about God's relationship with them in this parable is conveyed in a loving, forgiving embrace. Hildegard of Bingen beautifully summarises, also in

---

5 See Margaret Lyall's (1997) helpful discussion on the comparison of tendencies to touching in therapy in her essay *The Pastoral Counselling Relationship: A Touching Place?*

6 Jesus touched many in order to bring healing and hope, for example, the crippled woman in Luke 13: 10–13, two blind men in Matthew 20: 29f and Jesus cleansing a leper in Luke 5: 16. He washed the feet of his friends, not just functionally to clean them but as a humble gesture of love in John 13. Jesus blessed the little children in Mark 10:1 3–16.
   Jesus was open to love and care being offered to him through touch, for example, his anointing at Bethany in Mark 14: 3–9.

7 Luke 15: 20.

an embodied image, God's attitude towards humanity, 'God hugs you, you are encircled by the arms of the mystery of God' (cited by Matthew Fox, 1983, 224).

The question for spiritual and pastoral carers is not whether to touch in caring relationships but who, when and how – a complex issue. The focus for the remainder of this chapter is how we may become increasingly self-aware about our sexuality, our embodied selves, and our attitudes to our bodies in order to unravel some of the complexities relating to touch as a therapeutic tool. For what essentially holds us back from touching another within a pastoral relationship when we sense it may be appropriate, is not our fear of misusing power or our touch being misconstrued as sexual harassment. Rather, it is our discomfort with our own embodied sexuality – not being comfortable in our own skin.

> For everything there is a season, and a time for every matter under heaven:
>
> a time to embrace and a time to refrain from embracing. . .[8]

Rory is a local Church of England vicar in his thirties who is married and in the first year of his first parish. At her request, he has begun to visit Victoria, a housebound single woman in her late fifties, every couple of months, to share the Eucharist. Usually, Yvonne, a member of the congregation and Victoria's pastoral visitor, participates, too. Victoria has lived with multiple sclerosis for more than ten years and in the last few months has been increasingly confined to her home. As he shares communion with the two women, their fingers and hands often touch and as they share the Peace, Rory shakes both of their hands warmly with one hand and places his other hand on top of the women's wrists or hands. Six months after their first shared communion, Yvonne unexpectedly has to look after her son who has been sent home from school the afternoon

---

8   Ecclesiastes 3 1 and 5b.

they are due at Victoria's. Rory telephones Victoria to see if she would like to re-arrange their visit, but she says would really like communion today as she has been feeling low recently.

When Rory arrives, Victoria is in her bed (usually she is sitting in a wheelchair in the living room), wearing a nightdress with a cardigan over it. She doesn't look particularly well. Victoria's care giver has been in to give her some lunch, but most of it is still on a tray on a bedside cabinet. Rory is a little disconcerted by being in Victoria's bedroom alone, but senses Victoria is anxious to proceed with communion. As usual, Rory shakes Victoria warmly by the hand at the sharing of the Peace, but he notices Victoria holds on for longer than usual. As Rory lets go of her hand, Victoria begins to cry. She then begins to tell Rory how his handshake and Yvonne's cuddle during communion are one of the few times in the last months, even years, that anyone touches her in a non-functional way. Her carers help her dress, toilet and bathe, and they are usually gentle in doing so, a couple of her friends give her a perfunctory kiss at the beginning and end of a visit, and she hardly ever sees her only brother who lives in Canada. Right now she feels so alone and frightened. As she is sitting up in her bed with her head off her pillows, Rory instinctively bends forward and gives Victoria a cuddle. She sobs in his arms and does not let go for over a minute.

On his way home Rory wonders if he has done the right thing for Victoria and for himself. Over the evening meal, he talks it through with his with wife and the following week he does the same with his pastoral supervisor.

Hunter and Struve (1998, cited by Litchfield, 2006, 103) have developed several categories of touch which are part of a continuum. It will be helpful for us to look at the above case study within this framework. The forms of touch they describe are:

- accidental: for example, brushing against someone, as Rory, Yvonne and Victoria's fingers did as they shared bread and wine

- task-orientated: functional, as Victoria described the touch of her carers
- attentional: to gain or hold attention, for example alerting someone to their turn, touch involved in a greeting or farewell, such as Victoria's friends' perfunctory kisses
- celebratory/affectional: expressing positive regard, nurturing, comforting. Rory may have hoped this was conveyed in his handshake at the sharing of the Peace and perhaps also in his embrace of Victoria in response to her distress. Perhaps Victoria interpreted Rory's handshake and/or embrace in this way
- emotional/expressive: to convey gratitude, to protect, to offer emotional support. Rory may have intended his embrace to express emotional support and Victoria may have received it in this guise
- aggressive: impulsive, disregards boundaries and may cause physical harm
- sensual: for example, soothing caresses or tender embrace (without sexual stimulation) within an intimate relationship, between close relatives or friends. Rory as a male probably would not have seen his embrace in these terms but Victoria, as a female, might have[9]
- sexual: communicates overt or implied sexual interest or intention. This is what Rory feared Victoria might have misinterpreted his cuddle – as him taking advantage of her vulnerability in a sexual manner.

Rory was very clear about the intent informing his embrace of Victoria – to comfort and show compassion and support. Rory's sexual relationship with his wife was warm, loving

---

9 Men in general tend to seek to want to genitally sexualise an intimate relationship more than women. Sensual touching for men may commonly be interpreted as a prelude to overt sexual intimacy, whereas for women sensual touch is often enjoyed and taken as such with no sexual overtones. See Lichfield (2006) for a fuller discussion of the issue of sexuality, boundaries and touch.

and satisfying, and his parents had been tactile, caring and approachable in his developing years. In short, Rory was aware he hadn't cuddled Victoria as a means to seek compensation for a lack of physical affection in his own life. He strongly felt his actions had not been an abuse of power. However, during pastoral supervision, he realised how open he had made himself for his gesture to be misconstrued, especially as his embrace had been made in private and in Victoria's bedroom. His action was positively responded to – even though he hadn't asked Victoria if she had wanted a cuddle, she had clung on to him. However, did this meet her spiritual and pastoral needs (as intended), her sensual and/or indeed her sexual needs (in part)?

Three weeks later, Rory received a phone call from Victoria's carer. Victoria was now in hospital and she wondered if Rory and Yvonne could come and share the Eucharist with her. The next day, Rory and Yvonne went to see Victoria. At the sharing of the Peace, Yvonne automatically lent forward and gave Victoria a kiss and a hug. Rory followed suit and kissed Victoria on the cheek and gently squeezed both her shoulders. Victoria smiled at them both and thanked them for being such good friends. She died a week later.

Not all touch which conveys comfort or emotional support, of course, need be an embrace. A holding of a hand, a touch on a forearm or squeeze of a shoulder can convey similar sentiments. However, touching involves risk – the risk of getting it wrong, of being rejected. We can ask another if they would like their hand held or a cuddle, where it feels appropriate. Placing our hand and forearm on a bed or the arm of a chair can be a means of offering touch should the other person wish to reach out. If we get it wrong or are in doubt about our actions, it is important to reflect on our practice like Rory, as well as asking ourselves whose need was really being met in those circumstances.

As well as learning from reflection on previous experience, our ability to sensitively use touch as a therapeutic resource within caring relationships depends to a large degree on our discernment. It may be helpful when deciding whether or not to touch another in a caring relationship to consider the following scenarios where it is advisable to refrain from touching:[10]

- When the carer does not want to touch, or feel comfortable to touch, for whatever reason. A lack of genuineness or discomfort in touching will be picked up by the recipient.
- When the patient or parishioner's body language indicates they do not want to be touched.
- When touch would prematurely end emotional expression or deeper exploration of an issue to meet the carer's need. This may be due to the carer's discomfort and a wish to avoid further exposure to high expressed emotion or to the topic under consideration.
- When touch would encourage the patient or parishioner to avoid exploring difficult issues more deeply and/or be content with infantile gratification.
- When the carer feels manipulated by the patient or parishioner.
- When the carer is aware of the temptation to manipulate the patient or parishioner.

In order to help the reader reflect more deeply on their own attitude to, and use of touch in their own practice, the following questions are offered for consideration:

- Why do you touch others in pastoral relationships (or not)?
- How do you benefit from touching others in caring relationships?
- How do you feel about touching?
- Why?

---

10 These scenarios are based on a schema created by Margaret Lyall (1997), originally for pastoral counsellors.

Who do you feel comfortable/uncomfortable touching:

- People of the same gender, sexual orientation or age (younger or older)?
- People of a different gender, sexual orientation or age (older or younger)?
- Why?
- Where do you usually touch patients and parishioners?

Does where you touch others differ according to their gender, sexual orientation or age? If so, why?

Part II
Exploring Self

5

Relational Self

Perhaps, the person we find most challenging to comprehend at different times in our lives is ourselves: our patterns of behaviour, ways of relating, our feelings and our desires as well as where these originate from and why. This chapter offers some signposts to help pastors reflect a little deeper on the unconscious aspect of our being; how our degree of willingness to embrace its contents and our awareness of the opportunities afforded to us to glimpse and understand what it contains, influences our ways of relating. In addition, how relationships with authority figures, at home and in church, in our formative years significantly shape our behaviour and the interpersonal dynamics at play in caring relationships in the present is explored.

Our Relationship with our Unconscious Self

and what I would avoid, I carry with me, always.
John Burnside's poem Suburbs (2006, 2)

One particular facet of our human makeup which is formidable for any of us to relate to in a life-enhancing manner is what the Swiss psychologist Carl Jung referred to as our shadow. The shadow as defined by Frieda Fordham:

is the personal unconscious; it is all those uncivilized desires and emotions that are incompatible with social standards and our ideal personality, all that we are ashamed of, all that we do not want to know about ourselves. (1966, 50)

As Scots writer John Burnside observes, all that disgusts and frightens us about ourselves which we try to reject or deny as part of our makeup is something that is carried with us wherever we are or whatever we do. We cannot escape from it. 'Jung called the shadow, "the thing a person has no wish to be," "the sum of all those unpleasant qualities" from which one attempts to hide' (Ulanov and Dueck, 2008, 15 citing Jung 1966). The shadow is composed of the opposite of all that spiritual and pastoral carers are conventionally trained and expected to be: possessing aggressive, egocentric, competitive and manipulative urges rather than calm, altruistic, compassionate and transparent ways of being (Sandford, 1992). Robert Bly, an American poet, uses the image of a rubbish bag into which we deposit repressed emotions and unwanted dimensions of our personality to describe our shadow (Monbourquette, 2001). It is quite literally the baggage we carry with us that weighs us down and impinges on our quality of life and our relationships.

The contents of our shadow are far from being inert and inactive. It takes a significant amount of emotional energy to attempt to repress and contain such threatening and culturally non-acceptable feelings and personality traits in our personal unconscious. Despite such effort, the contents of our shadow bubble up and leak out in unintentional and often unexpected ways as we relate to others. The shadow contains material which cannot be simply be discarded but requires to be intentionally sifted through and consciously owned to be less burdensome. Contrary to popular belief, it is not an exploration of such repressed culturally inappropriate desires and feelings that facilitates a living out of, for example, sexual predilections or fantasies. It is quite the opposite. Wilkie Au and Noreen Cannon , who have written widely on the relationship between Christian spirituality and depth psychology, explain further:

> Acting out stems from unconscious. Consciousness gives us choice and makes us able to respond in a deliberate

way, according to our moral and ethical principles. It is when we split off from our instincts that we are most in danger of acting them out. The aim of consciousness is self-discovery and personal responsibility. The more we know about our own human instincts and desires, the more responsibly we can live. (Au and Cannon, 1995, 28)

We cannot wipe out our shadow or cut it adrift. To recognize our basic drives and deep-seated feelings and become more whole and emotionally healthy people we need to understand and integrate them. As W. H. Auden (in his poem *Song for St Cecelia's Day II*) implies, our shadows are paradoxically difficult to confront but if we dare venture there, they are places of opportunity for profound ongoing learning:

> I cannot grow
> I have no shadow
> To run away from (cited by Mendelson 1979a, 97)

Unfortunately, significant theological understandings and ecclesial structures within the Christian tradition have encouraged many pastors and church workers to run away from the shadow and resist such an embracing of the darker side to our human makeup. Thus, reinforcing that socially and morally inappropriate desires and urges are to be suppressed and supplanted. The most widely publicized example in recent times of the dangers of this approach to dealing with such proclivities has been the sexual abuse of youngsters by celibate male clergy.

On a more positive note, the shadow potentially contributes significantly to who we are as whole persons rooted in the reality of life and living, as well as adding colour and vim and vigour to our personhood and relationships. The fullness of God's creation includes night and day, darkness and light.

In the darkness God created light, order emerged from chaos.[1] From the darkness, light and hope and integration can come. Simon Bailey was a gay Anglican priest who kept a journal of his struggles to come to terms with his sexuality. His sister utilized his journals to write his biography after his death:

> 'Is there a gay love for Christ?' He [Simon] began to see that his homosexuality was not necessarily a burden and wrote in his journal, 'I have a deep wound, a kind of flaw at the centre . . . it can in itself be turned into a glory. . .' But, he asked himself, 'Can I really explore the shadows the way I do and still carry the light for people? I think maybe there would be no light without the shadows. People think priests are pure and holy – most honest priests know more about the shadows than anything else'. (Bailey 1997, 19–20)

Ignoring or sidelining our shadow is to lead a less-than-full, congruous and honest life and, thus, is to offer less than best possible pastoral and spiritual care. Exploring it requires courage and integrity but may lead to new possibilities and ways of being. The type of openness to his personal unconscious that Simon Bailey displayed in his journal is also important as it grounds us in the reality that we are human and not anything more or less, with urges, desires and instincts to live and deal with like the people we seek to care for. Furthermore, John Sandford (1992), a psychologist and Anglican priest, insightfully suggests that those who seek to suppress their shadow tend to lack a sense of humour. Whatever we need in order to provide sensitive care, it is certainly an ability to live lightly with ourselves and the human predicament in general!

How can we identify our shadow? How can we recognize the signals and messages it gifts us so we can take note of, and learn

---

1   Genesis 1: 1–5.

from, them if we choose? Here, three significant ways in which the shadow can be observed in our lives will be briefly explored.[2]

Projection

Significantly, the unloved and rejected aspects of ourselves can be glimpsed when a strength of emotion is aroused within us disproportionate to the action of another or the circumstances in which these feelings are felt.

John, in his mid-thirties, was the team leader in a local ecumenical project. He worked with four other church workers, from a variety of different denominations. Each had a job description, in which it was clearly stated that John had management responsibility for the team. In the main John's approach was collaborative and encouraging of his colleagues. John, however, did have a tendency to take on too much and it was a standing joke in the team that he was late for everything. Upon the departure of one of the team, a new member was appointed, in his fifties, whose tendency was to do his own thing without consultation with John or the others. Everyone in the team was struggling with Ben's behaviour and attitude and John had raised the issue with him. John had also said to the rest of the team to let Ben settle in and to wait and see if his conversation with Ben made a difference. Four months after his appointment, Ben arrived 15 minutes late for the weekly team meeting (ten minutes after John), carrying a coffee from a nearby café. As Ben sat down, John erupted, 'Late and no coffee for the rest of us . . . typical!' As he embarked on a rant

---

2 The three ways outlined in this chapter that offer us opportunities to notice how our shadow enters our consciousness are less intentional than some of the methods outlined by authors such as Au and Cannon (1995) and Monbourquette (2001). For example, Au and Cannon (1995, 42) suggest readers describe the personality traits and qualities of the two sons in the parable of the prodigal son (Luke 15: 11–32). They then ask with which of the two sons we might identify and which seems the opposite of who we are. The son with whom we do not identify represents aspects of our shadow.

outlining a litany of complaints against Ben, John felt his face redden and his body shake, such was his fury.

John was glad of his monthly supervision session at the end of the week where he could begin to explore what his outburst had really been about, such was its intensity. With some gentle prodding from his supervisor, John began to realize there was a pattern to the way he dealt with anger. He tended to think of himself as a pretty easy-going person but recently at home, life had rather challenging too. His wife had just returned to work after maternity leave following the birth of their second child. Everyone was dealing with a new routine and not all that much sleep was being had. Neither John nor his wife liked to row but he felt he was being asked to juggle an awful lot at home, and now at work Ben was being unreasonable. Judith, his wife, had spontaneously treated herself to a new outfit the previous week for a forthcoming family wedding and John felt they couldn't really afford it – the car needed servicing and they all badly needed a holiday. She had said John's look could have killed when he saw her bring her bags into the house when she returned from the shops. A couple of doors were slammed but few words exchanged.

With further encouragement, John began to talk about his family of origin and the way they dealt with anger. As his supervisor helped John to especially explore his father's behaviour patterns in relation to anger, John could begin to see that he was mirroring what he, as a child, had observed his father enacting. Feelings were seldom explicitly expressed and if his mother and father argued, doors were banged, pots rattled in the sink, grips on newspapers tightened and then his father went to the allotment. Occasionally, the pressure cooker exploded and John vividly remembered his father throwing a glass against the kitchen wall. However, such outbursts were rare.

Over the next few supervisory sessions, John began to develop more helpful strategies to help him express his anger in his working and personal lives as well as look at how he and the rest of the team might improve their internal communications. Not only that, John was also able to identify during supervision part of what he found difficult working with Ben – he could perceive something of himself in Ben's patterns of behaviour, especially his tendency to work to his own timescale and leave everyone else waiting for him to arrive for meetings or prior to Sunday worship.

John was genuinely angry and frustrated at Ben's behaviour, but a longstanding suppression of what he had absorbed as a child in relation to negative or socially unacceptable feelings and the public expression of these feelings, had also been released and vented at Ben. In addition, John's built up resentment and irritation at what had been happening recently at home was also transferred onto Ben. Significantly, up until then, John had disowned his poor timekeeping – behaviour he had repeatedly refused to face up to – by projecting it onto his colleague. Projection involves a disliked element of ourselves being displaced onto another and treating that aspect of ourselves as their problem (Carr 2008). In the main, we do so unconsciously. When such projection occurs, a disproportionately strong feeling is either explicitly expressed or internally felt, perhaps somatically, a sign that something significant is going on in our unconscious. If we are able to stop and listen to the blame and criticism we have for another (either verbalized or thought and both accompanied by underlying feeling), then we will learn much about ourselves. Priest and psychologist John Monbourquette quotes Wilber (1982) to help underline this:

> Our carping criticisms of other people are really nothing but unrecognised bits of autobiography. If you want to know what a person is really like, listen to what he says about other people. (2001, 87)

Likewise, when we feel an urge to deify or heap praise on another, they may possess qualities or attributes which we inherently possess but yet do not realize or consciously own.

The Old Testament tale of David's blindness to his sexual covetousness until it is revealed by the prophetic storytelling of Nathan is a classic example of the shadow side of an individual being exposed by the wise and honest support of another.[3] David added beautiful Bathsheba to his already extensive harem and had her husband Uriah placed on a battlefield where he would most certainly be slain. David reacts with great anger when Nathan tells him of the story of a powerful rich man who already possesses large flocks and herds yet steals a poor man's only lamb. Nathan in response tells David he is that man. To David's credit, he realizes the awfulness of his attitude and actions and appeals to God for forgiveness. He consciously takes ownership of a despicable aspect of his unconscious makeup and is able to take measures to change.

Scapegoating

In the build up to the 2010 football World Cup in South Africa, England were perceived, at least in the media, to have a good chance of progressing far into the competition, if not winning it outright. In England's first game, their performance was disappointing and the result even more so – they drew a goal apiece with USA, who they were expected to beat. Unfortunately, the goal England conceded was due to basic error by their goalkeeper Robert Green. Despite later making a save that kept his team in the game, Green was lambasted in the British media for his high-profile gaff. In addition, he was dropped from the England team for the rest of the competition.

Such scapegoating by identifying and designating a particular person or group as problematic and projecting onto them responsibility for the failures or frustrations of a nation, community, family or, in this case, a team is far from a contemporary phenomenon. Since biblical times, where Old Testament

---

3   2 Samuel 12: 1-15

prophets and Jesus himself were scapegoats, through to Jewish and gypsy communities and disabled and homosexual individuals being scapegoated in Nazi Germany, such a means of dealing with our collective shadow has been utilized.

> On a cultural level, the shadow means what our group, our tribe, our religion, our political party deems negative, out of bounds, to be shunned, to be improved, or to be punished. Behind every social oppression lurks a piece of group shadow whose members are exporting it onto others who are not of their tribe. (Ulanov and Dueck, 2008, 56)

In church, local community and hospital settings, scapegoating is a common phenomenon which we too can frequently participate in, either as an active contributor or as a recipient. The open and questioning member of a committee who raises the uncomfortable issues in meetings but always seems to get the blame if decisions don't get quickly made or the meeting drags on. The introvert consultant physician in the hospital ward who is less inclined to be collaborative in decision-making and tends to get the brunt of general ill-feeling when outcomes for patients are poor. For example, if discharge planning goes wrong and an individual has to be re-admitted quickly or if active treatment has been prolonged when a patient might have received more palliative care earlier, enabling them to die with some dignity in their place of choice. 'The feeling tone is, "If it weren't for that misfit, everything in our group would be fine"' (Au and Cannon, 1995, 36).

It is important, once aware of such scapegoating, to ask ourselves what the underlying issues are and why we may be contributing. Likewise, if we sense we are being made a scapegoat, it may help us to realize that there are collective frustrations and dis-ease around, for which we are not entirely responsible. Such awareness may prevent us personally absorbing and inappropriately bearing the load of the projected feelings of a group or community and enables us to begin to take appropriate remedial action. If such shadow material is not faced it may be absorbed into our unconscious and, thus, has potential to influence our behaviour. There is the danger, therefore, that repeated unchallenged scapegoating from those we relate closely to can lead us or another to act out that which is being collectively projected onto us or them. Therefore, the questioning committee member may become truly pedantic and stubborn and the quiet physician more withdrawn and non-communicative.

Dreams and Fantasies

Our shadows are often revealed to us in our dreams – embodying a character of our own sex and the form of an unpleasant, repugnant or hostile character. If we take notice of the pattern of the internal dramas that enfold during our sleep we can learn much about what we fear, the desires we suppress and the reality of who we are. Attentiveness to fleeting daydreams and fantasies can also reveal much about our deepest urges and desires, which we have been socially conditioned to push into unconscious – flashes of sexual impulses, urges for violent outbursts or energizing moments of raw competitiveness. However, our nocturnal dreams and daytime fantasies do not just reveal negative instincts – heroic fantasies of great athletic prowess, performing altruistic feats or acts of justice may help us to rediscover our vocational path or inspire us to journey in a different direction. Journaling our dreams and exploring them with the help of a trained and trusted other can lead us to a deeper understanding of our unconscious selves. Some have found drawing, painting or sculpting their dreams, 'automatic' thoughts or images that fleetingly come to their mind's eye to be a source of great creativity.

Surrealist artists such as Rene Magritte, Jean Miro and Paul Delvaux from the 1920s onwards have found that such modes of artistic expression enabled their unconscious selves to be represented in their work. 'This kind of painting was, in theory, the unfettered product of the unconscious mind, sidestepping old-fashioned aesthetic value judgements' (Elliott, 2010, 9). Surrealist art and sculpture often provokes a primal response from those who engage, with the erotic, violent, mystical and often contradictory images portrayed. Here, too, we can glimpse our shadow's presence and something of the suppressed energy in our unconscious as Surrealist art reads us or uncovers uncomfortable aspects within us, even as we seek to interpret it. Carl Jung himself drew and painted his dreams as a means of seeking to understand more fully his unconscious. There is more than a touch of the playful about this approach, which may be helpful to some of us in our ongoing integration of the darker side of who we are.

We will never fully integrate our shadow in this life but we can develop our awareness of how to become more familiar with it. As in the case of King David, Au and Cannon describe how seeking to make the contents of our shadow conscious can enable us to become more of the person God intends us to be:

> For as we look at what frightens and shames us and come to know the pain that made us reject ourselves in the first place, we become newly receptive to God's healing grace . . . As God's love for those wounded parts of us sinks in, we are able, perhaps for the first time, to love ourselves, dark side and all. We also find ourselves more able to reach out in love and compassion to others because we are less self-righteous and judgemental. (1995, 41)

Self in Relationship with Others

Humans are social beings. LaCugna, a Trinitarian theologian, is strident not only about God existing in relationship but about our need as human persons for relationships. 'To exist as a person is to be referred to others; the negation and dissolution of personhood is total self-reference' (1991, cited by

Pembroke, 2006, 11). We inherit genes which shape our physical appearance and leave us vulnerable to certain diseases and psychopathologies which may greatly influence our identities and self-perception. However, we are also shaped, formed and reformed in relationships. 'To be a person is to be in relationship' (Pembroke 2006, 11).

The Influence of Significant Relationships in Our Formative Years.

From adult authority figures in our early years, we learn which patterns of behaviour and ways of being and relating, will earn us affirmation and attention. These learnt models of interaction are then acted out in our adult relationships. 'Childhood scripts are like hypnotic suggestions that work beneath awareness to keep us stuck in the same process even though the characters and circumstances change' (Muse 2000, 254). Parental anxieties, ambitions and projections may have a significant influence on who and what we become, though as Andrew Grieg infers, we do have choice as to what extent we live out these in later life (if and when we become aware of whose needs we are living our lives according to):

> It is easy to mistake oneself. Families do it for you early on, friends assist you later (enemies tend to be more accurate; they get you). 'The quiet one', 'the wild one', 'the sensible one' – the labels are handed out and stick even as she is hollering within, and he yearns to be acceptable, and she is driven to be what she can never be.
>
> Pointless to blame others, you do it for yourself. They do not so much fuck you up, as give you a wrong account of yourself and let you do the rest. (Grieg, 2010, 98)

Potentially, those labels, attitudes and patterns of behaviour embedded deep within us from formative years which harm and hurt us, and others, can be transformed and unlearnt with appropriate support and much reflection and hard work. However, they can also be reinforced or re-emerge in certain contexts and relationships with perceived authority figures in the present. What is easier to write than do, is to neither listen to nor absorb destructive messages, and to remember that we have this choice. On the other hand, sometimes our families and friends do get their assessment of our character and behaviour right but we ignore their insights.

Many who take on vocational caring roles in adult life, such as spiritual and pastoral carers, do so bearing the emotional wounds from early childhood years. The extent to which we are aware of this has significance not only for the well-being of those we work with but also for ourselves. Stephen Muse explains further:

> To a young child of four or five, taking the blame for adult problems is standard operating procedure . . . the young child experiences him or herself as the centre of the universe. The parents' emotional and physical safety is instinctively experienced as important as one's own. The sense of where the parent ends and the child begins emotionally is not yet distinct. Thus, children will as a matter of course sacrifice their own emotional life to help their parents' survive. (2000, 256)

If the pastor or spiritual carer has not had, or taken, the opportunity to deepen their understanding of their internal life which has been shaped by their formative relationships, what is carried from their childhood unconscious caring into a parish or institutional context will be used unconsciously to meet the carer's – not primarily the parishioners' or patients' – deep-seated needs within pastoral relationships. From within an American context, Harbaugh helpfully says:

> Seminarians often bring to their studies some heavy burdens from early life, experiences with the family and

sometimes with the church . . . Since so little time is
spent in seminary with the healing of hurtful memories
of the past, it is probable that most of the seminarian's
'unfinished business' is taken into the parish. (cited by
Capps, 1993, 9)

Rita was a hardworking hospital chaplain in her forties who
was well liked and respected within the large acute hospital
where she had worked for seven years. Her senior male colleague tended to do most of the strategic planning, relate
closely with hospital management, be involved in several
local and national committees associated to psycho-spiritual
and bereavement care, and was also in demand to lecture on
these issues. Rita, on the other hand, tended to get on with
the regular visiting around the hospital's wards and units, and
increasingly hospital staff sought her out for support – professional, personal and ritual. By the time every holiday came
round, Rita was always shattered and she spent the first seven to
ten days recuperating before she felt energized to enjoy herself,
and her family were able to enjoy her. Her husband remarked
every year that she was a different woman for the last three or
four days of her fortnight summer break and there were frequent tensions in their marriage relationship about the hours
Rita worked. Rita's senior colleague repeatedly recommended
that she find herself a supervisor to help her regularly review
her work pattern and content. Rita, however, always found a
reason not to enter into such a relationship; there never seemed
to be right person around for her to relate to as a supervisor,
the chaplaincy budget couldn't stretch to it and so on. Finally,
even her children began to resent her weariness, short temper
and lack of spark in the evenings and during her weekends off.
Finally, Rita went to her doctor burnt out and depressed. She
was immediately signed off work and at that point acting on
the doctor's advice, Rita went for some counselling.

Rita was resistant at first to talk with the counsellor about
her formative years. She always felt she had had the benefit

of a secure childhood, neither of her parents were absent or drunk much, and she never was hit or shouted at; talking about her parents in any negative sense seemed disloyal. However, with her husband's support and her doctor's insight and encouragement, Rita persisted with counselling. Over the weeks, Rita's story unfolded – she had a very outgoing, bright and handsome older brother who was the apple of her parents' eye. He was nine years older than Rita and was very sociable – even as a small girl she remembered him having friends to sleep over and big birthday parties. However, as a teenager he was wild – his parents never knew where he was, who he was with, what he was indulging in and if the police were going to bring him home. Rita at a young age had to act as peacekeeper – placating her parents' anxieties, being good and diligent in her timekeeping and schoolwork. She was the one that was always there, appeasing and calming. The only time, Rita recalled she got much parental attention and affirmation was when she got good marks at school and when she was chosen to play the violin in the school orchestra (both of which involved lots of hard work because Rita didn't consider herself particularly academically or musically gifted).

As she explored her current patterns of behaviour further with the counsellor, Rita realized she was still grafting to gain affirmation and maintain her sense of self-worth. Her deep-seated need to receive attention and reduce anxiety as an ever-present calming and reassuring presence for others disabled Rita's ability to lead a balanced life, including meeting her own physical and spiritual need for rest and relaxation as well as the needs of her husband and family. Rita also realized she was also, at times, still appeasing authority figures for the behaviour of her 'big brother' when colleagues from other healthcare disciplines couldn't contact her boss in the hospital as he was in a meeting or lecturing elsewhere. Rita realized her resentment of her senior colleague manifested itself in obstructive behaviour, such as not following up his recommendations to find a supervisor, and had its roots in deep-seated anger, not just at her brother but at her parents for not affirming her as she would have wished. The manner in which she was expressing this anger was detrimental not just to the dynamics of the chaplaincy team, but also ultimately to her.

In general terms, understanding (as Freud proposed) that key childhood relationships still unconsciously inform our adult ones, especially with authority figures, is important for pastoral and spiritual carers. We continue to transfer feelings and attitudes, most often from relationships with authority figures in our early years onto others we deem to have status and power in the present (and, similarly, others do so onto us when we offer them spiritual or pastoral care, as explored later in this chapter). For example, Rita does this with healthcare managers and, to some extent, with her chaplaincy colleague. Likewise, patients and parishioners may give form and meaning to relationships with ourselves, as pastors, that originate from their childhood.[4]

Thomas Merton insightfully reflects on the behaviour of those of us whose ways of relating, like Rita, are significantly informed by harmful unconscious childhood scripts which drive us to find affirmation and a sense of worth through our work:

> You are probably striving to build yourself an identity in your work, out of your work and your witness. You are using it so to speak, to protect yourself against nothingness, annihilation. This is not the right use of work. (cited by Shannon, 1985, in Muse, 2000, 258)

As well as developing and holding onto a theology which means we do not have to define ourselves by what we do to feel of worth, life-enhancing and helpful models of relating to others and self may also be absorbed from influential persons

---

4   For a fuller exploration of the nuances of transference see for example: Barrie Hinksman (1999) and Wesley Carr (2008).

in our childhood, which may enable us to thrive in adult relationships. If we are fortunate to find ourselves in loving, trusting and affirming relationships as children, we are more likely to risk revealing our inner selves in later relationships. In such adult relationships built on mutual trust and respect, we may rediscover aspects of our personhood forgotten, suppressed or discarded and discover dimensions we never knew we had. Stanley Kunitz was 90 when he asked of his wife in his poem *Touch Me*:

> Darling, do you remember
> the man you married? Touch me
> remind me who I am. (1995, 158)

It is in positive, mutually enhancing relationships that we are able to live into the process of who and what we are becoming and learn from the hardships, losses and gifts of life experienced along the way. In Jonathan Coe's novel about growing up in the 1970s Britain, *The Rotters' Club*, Benjamin, the story's central character, writes a critical review of his school production of Othello and its female lead, Cicely (to whom he is very attracted), in the school magazine. Subsequently, Benjamin feels guilty about what this may have done for Cicely's self-worth and this impedes his ability to relate to her in any meaningful way. Years later, after they have left school and Benjamin discovers his feelings for Cicely are reciprocated, the couple discuss the motivation for, and implications of, his critique.

> 'How can you forgive me?'
> 'Forgive you? Forgive you for what?'
> 'For writing that review.'
> 'But, Benjamin – that was simply ages ago.'
> 'Yes, I know that; but still – it was so hurtful. So unkind.'

'Not at all. I've told you this before; it was the best thing anyone could have done for me. I was never any good at acting.
I was just doing it because my mother wanted me to, and
because it fitted in with some stupid self-image I had. You
cured me of that. That's what it was, literally; a cure. And
I don't believe you did it out of malice. You were already
writing music out of . . . out of love for me – I know that
now – and I think that's why you wrote the review, as well.'

'Out of love?'

'Yes, I think so. To show me to myself. That's what love
is, if you like. It's a condition in which . . . in which people help each other to see the truth about themselves.'
(2008, 354)

To enable us to mature, grow and be the individuals God
intends us to fully be, we need the support, guidance, integrity, wisdom and, above all else, the love of trusted others.
Such a process is impossible in isolation. It is in such relationships, where at times we may bruise or let the other down
without fear of rejection, we can become more aware of our
childhood scripts and the impact of early authority figures
on our lives in the present. Perhaps, too, with support, we
may rewrite any ingrained harmful dominant storylines or at
least lessen their unwanted impact on our current patterns of
behaviour.

Self in Relationship to
Our Formative Communities of Faith

Christian ethicists Stanley Hauerwas, a Methodist, and Sam
Wells, an Anglican, propose that in relationship with God,
we have the ultimate gracious and loving, yet honest, friend
who through the gifts and resources that God bestows on the
Church, especially to enable worship, is able to help shape
the formation and development of our personhood and
behaviour:

what God wants is for his people to worship him, to be his friends, and to eat with him; in short, to be his companions. The Eucharist offers a model of this companionship. Disciples gather and greet; are reconciled with God and one another; hear and share their common story; offer their needs and resources; remember Jesus and invoke his Spirit; and then share communion, before being sent out. Through worship – preparation, performance, repetition – God gives his people the resources they need to live in his presence. (Hauerwas and Wells, 2004, 13)

Belonging to such a community of faith provides structure and a ritual order to life, where, especially in our formative years, our values, beliefs and ways of relating are significantly sculpted. We learn not only about community, its creation and expression, 'In worship and the actions that flow from it, we also learn how to be Christians; and doing so we explore the nature and the claim of faith' (Forrester 1997, 46). Regular involvement in worship may provide foundations for, and stability in, life as well as the development of a framework through which and by which we engage with relational issues and moral decision-making in our adolescence and into adulthood. In addition, even at an early developmental stage with regular involvement in a community of faith, there are possibilities for transformation; what may be termed the 'conversion of life' (Faludy, 2006) or perhaps, for some, the conversion to life.[5] For others, however, our early experience in church may be far from life enhancing. Ecclesial authority

---

5   The hope is that it is an ongoing process and that learning and a yearning for ongoing transformation is a lifelong process. However, much depends on a youngster's experience of church and other familial, social and cultural factors in his or her life. There are, of course, local faith communities which do not encourage openness, questioning and growth in its members as well as individuals for whom further self-development or theological inquiry is either too threatening or not deemed to be relevant to a fuller life.

figures and dogma may loom large as significant life-limiting and deadening factors in formative and future years.

'We all have a ground, a place that secures and defines us' (Greig 2006a, 40). This may be where we lived as a child or stay as an adult (with or without a partner or family), our place of birth or the local community that we have grown to call home. However, for the pastoral carer, the community of faith in which we have been and actively are loved, nurtured, accepted and affirmed for who we are, in and of ourselves, is a key place that shapes and significantly defines us. It is the ground that secures and roots our identity. As Charles Gerkin puts it: 'To belong to that community (of faith) is to share in a life of ritual, prayer and action that continually reminds the members of a community who they are and who they are to be in the world' (1997, 110). The community of faith to which we belong is our narrative home, the community where the grand story we are heirs to is heard, eaten, sprinkled, sung, enacted and embodied. In that story-formed communal context, we may continue to interpret and re-interpret our individual stories (including our theology) as we reflect on our experience of life. How such possible ongoing reformation and transformation by being part of regular worship may inform our development as persons and pastors will be further explored in the last chapter of the book.

For now, the important question for us as carers is – how aware are we of the influence of our own formation in a local community of faith during our childhood? How has our early experience of church shaped our values, beliefs and attitudes? How have the relationships we experienced with authority figures in that community and the doctrine we absorbed through the attitudes and behaviours in the local church and the atmosphere in worship and at church related activities influenced us and our ways of relating, being and doing in the present?

In particular, for good or ill, our attitudes to issues of sexuality, sexual orientation and gender and approaches to conflict and anger management will have been influenced by our early church involvement (if we were involved as a youngster), not just by the parental messages we were exposed to. Scottish practical theologian Duncan Forrester, whilst exploring ecclesial ethics, offers an aspirational description of the impact of worship for regular participants at whatever stage in life we are at:

> In worship we receive a new identity, we are formed morally. By encountering God we learn how to be disciples. We learn to love by being loved; we learn to forgive by being forgiven; we learn generosity by being treated generously. (1997, 56)

Perhaps this statement offers a benchmark by which we can reflect on our own formative and present experience of being part of church worship and activities.

Socially Constructed Self

The construction and ongoing re-construction of our identities is a complex issue. Undoubtedly, we carry with us our own personal and professional self-images and our own perceptions of what a pastor or spiritual carer embodies, informed by theological reflection on personal experience and professional practice. Our identities are also socially constructed through exposure to familial, ecclesial, local community and national cultures. 'Self understanding is inevitably shaped by the warp and woof of the threads that represent the particular narrative of an individual's experience and its social context' (Ramsay, 2004, 166). Who we feel we are and our perceptions about the various roles we enact in our personal and professional lives, have been and continue to be, influenced by the attitudes and judgements of influential others in our past and in the present. Thus, our identities and our roles in life are negotiated, socially constructed, with others. People invest meanings in us as theological students, ministers, chaplains and church workers over which we have no control. We are different things to different people in varying contexts and at different times. Being aware of such potential for transference and projection is crucial to enable sensitive care to be offered. What we can explore more deeply is our response (internal and external) to them (countertransference), utilizing such reflective tools as supervision, mentorship and journaling. A starting point for such engagement is asking ourselves *what did this encounter say about me* rather than what is the matter with the parishioner or patient? A second important question to ask is *whose need was really being met in that exchange?*

Shortly after being appointed to my first chaplaincy post, I was asked by the nursing staff in the neurosurgical unit to see a 39-year-old shipbuilder who had recently been diagnosed with an aggressive, inoperable brain tumour. Bob's considerable, yet understandable, distress was rendering his family and the ward staff helpless and upset. Could I offer him some support? On approaching Bob and introducing myself, I was met at first by stony silence and then by a very angry man who told me in no uncertain terms to get out of his sight. I retreated somewhat sheepishly. However, the next day I decided to try again, this time whilst his family were present. Bob roared at me before I could utter a greeting – I could take my God elsewhere because God was no use to him (or words to that effect!).

Active treatment was not an option for Bob and he went home soon after to the care of his own doctor and palliative care services. I never saw Bob again. However, I did see his wife. Ironically, she came over to the chaplaincy centre later that day to apologize for Bob's behaviour. However, it gave me the opportunity to apologize to her because I realized I had far from offered person-centred care – I had not respected Bob's wishes and had invaded his privacy. In short, I felt guilty because I felt I had added to his distress and had not acted in Bob's best interests. However, Jean graciously brushed aside my apology and began to talk. She needed to express her despair, sense of hopeless, struggle with lack of control and all her anxiety about the uncertainty of what the future may hold for Bob, herself and the rest of the family. Jean also spontaneously told me something of Bob's story. It transpired Bob was originally from the Western Isles of Scotland and had been brought up in a familial and church culture where he absorbed the understanding that good things happened to those who were hard working and faithful to God and the wicked got what they deserved. On leaving school, Lewis and its restrictive Calvinistic church culture, Bob came to Glasgow to do his apprenticeship. In his early twenties, he met Jean, they fell in love and got married. Unfortunately, their first child had died in infancy. This hit Bob hard. The local minister had been very supportive of Jean at the time but Bob would have nothing to do with him. After Jean had finished recounting their shared life together with all its ups and downs and her struggle at times to deal with Bob's occasional angry outbursts, I suggested Jean might like some support from her local minister in the days ahead. Not to invade Bob's space but to enable her to have someone outside the family to talk to about her concerns. Jean welcomed this. She had heard of the minister, Alice, by repute, and it was agreed that I phone Alice to alert her to Jean's situation. I was then able to set up an introductory meeting with Jean and Alice in the chaplaincy prior to Bob's discharge.

A few months later Alice rang me to tell me that Bob had died in the local hospice, still angry and full of existential questions, but less so than in the immediacy of his diagnosis. She was still seeing Jean regularly, in the manse, not in her home. Bob had known that Jean was getting support from Alice but he did not want her in his house. Bob had requested a Humanist funeral but Jean was now planning a short memorial service for Bob with Alice's help to be held in the church.

I can only surmise about the real source of Bob's anger directed at me. The first time we met, his anger was not about me as a human being but was about me being a chaplain (the second time, he would undoubtedly have been angry at me ignoring his initial request and yet his rage was disproportionate to this). Bob probably transferred his deep-seated feelings about his oppressive religious upbringing onto me as a perceived representative of the Church. In addition to representing ecclesial (and perhaps familial) authority figures from the past, I assume I also embodied for him an unjust, cruel and judgemental God who he perhaps deemed responsible for the hugely significant loss of his first child, now his own identity and, very soon, his life. All of this, of course, is only speculation.

However, with supervision what I came to realize was that my second visit to Bob was more about meeting my needs than his. Here, referring to one of five aspects of American pastoral theologian Pamela Cooper-White's method for reflection on pastoral encounters is enlightening. It requires:

> An examination of *countertransference in the classical sense* (from Freud) as one's own "unfinished business" and tender spots in one's own personal history that might distort or impede an empathic understanding of the other's reality. (2006, 234)

Here my own need to be needed, to find self-worth in making a difference by performing well and rescuing another from a dire situation in part contributed to my desire to return to see Bob for a second time. Yes, Bob exhibited spiritual distress but he in no uncertain terms rejected my offer of help. What drove me back to visit again? Perhaps in part, a desire to help alleviate such distress. Yet, in addition, there is no doubt I was enacting a deeply embedded script absorbed in my childhood. I was just in post, trying to establish a credibility with colleagues from different disciplines, trying to make a difference and I had failed. I had been rejected and I needed to go back again to prove my worth.

Helpfully, Cooper-White also challenges pastors to reflect on 'one's own *countertransference in the contemporary sense*' (2006, 234) as part of her method for pastoral reflection.[6] Here we are to reflect on the intersubjective dynamic of what happened in the present moment of the encounter, not a transfer of feelings and behaviours from the past which may distort or inhibit care. In this respect, what fantasies, associations, thoughts and feelings are glimpsed arising from unconscious in the present for the carer as we seek to respond to the patient or parishioner. For me, in retrospect, what I saw in Bob was possibly myself. Though ten years younger at the time, I had two children and, as a junior doctor and now as a chaplain, I had often fantasized about how I would deal with a terminal illness or the sudden death of a loved one. I would rage like Dylan Thomas, and Bob, and I would rage against God. I sometimes felt angry with God about the living hell of the situations I found patients and relatives in and like the psalmist asked God, why?[7] Maybe, in part at some level, I went a second time to normalize Bob's feelings – to say to Bob it's okay to rage, it's okay to be angry with God, and as a human being and God's representative so am damn well I! If it were happening to me I would be more than angry, too. I wanted to say, 'It's not fair, it's not just, so give it to God in the neck big time!' Perhaps, I went back for a second visit because if Bob was me, I would have wanted to rant at God and I wanted to give him that chance, whether that was the reality for Bob or not.

---

6 Cooper-White's (2006) pastoral method of reflecting on practice includes 1) self-care, 2) an examination of our countertransference in the Freudian sense, 3) an assessment of the other's pastoral needs, 4) examination of our countertransference in the contemporary sense and 5) theological reflection.

7 Psalm 74: 1.

6

*Vulnerable Self**

There is a crack in everything – that's how the light gets in.
Leonard Cohen (from the song Anthem, 1992)

To be human is to be vulnerable; it is to know the experience of having cracks, being cracked open and fear breaking
completely. Yet, paradoxically, it is through our woundedness
and imperfection that hope and light might not only be glimpsed
but grace shared in the caring relationships we form with others.

Woundedness is not just what others and life inflict on us.
We are not mere victims of tragedy and transition; many of
our wounds are, at least in part, caused by ourselves. The contemporary hymn writer Brian Wren captures this aspect of
our vulnerability in these penitential words:

> We come with self-inflicted pains
> of broken trust and chosen wrong,
> half free, half bound by inner chains. . .
> (2005, 484)

In addition, vulnerability is more than just what is already
part of our story. 'Vulnerability may indicate woundedness
from the past, or it may indicate a willingness to be wounded
in the present or the future' (Bennett Moore, 2002, 124).

---

* Chapters six, seven and eight cover a range of over-lapping and intimately
related aspects of our personhood which significantly inform our relating and
way of being – our human vulnerability, limitations and mortality. These fea-
tures are essential for any spiritual and pastoral carer to have at least tentatively
begun to explore, if not, in part, own. By doing so, we may be more able to
allow others to be as they need to be in the face of these issues in their lives and
feel comfortable enough to explore them with our help. Each of us as carers,
like those we care for, is vulnerable, limited and mortal.

To be vulnerable and risk exposure to fv
cracking is to follow Christ's example. R
St Julian and the Leper describes a comp'
of self not just to infection, distasteful c
cule in caring for a leper, but also to the ris.
deepening wounds of isolation, rejection and aba.
(in this case by the dispersing local community). Such lovi..
tenderness and steadfastness is to incarnate a willingness to be
vulnerable, to be Christ-like:

> Though all ran from him, he did not
> Run, but awaited
> Him with his arms
> Out, his ears stopped
> To his bell, his alarmed
> Crying. He lay down
> With him there, sharing his sores'
> Stench, the quarantine
> Of his soul; contaminating
> Himself with a kiss,
> With the love that
> Our science has disinfected. (1986, 99)

From the moment of our conception, in the journey from
womb to tomb, we live constantly with vulnerability – physical, emotional, spiritual and social. Made of flesh and bone,
we are not just susceptible to bruising and breakage, but to
inevitable decay, death and eventual decomposition. The
joy of love, friendship and fulfilment in relationships, work
and leisure means experiencing endings, loss and bereavement as part of living and relating in community. In growing
and developing, then ageing and maturing, we experience
transition and continual adjustment which exposes us to the
unknown and uncertain. All of these experiences leave us
susceptible to hurt, fear and loneliness, though (re)discover-
ing resources within and around us with, or without, the help

.se others help us to cope with, and sometimes, grow
ough such times.

The scars of such wounds are an ongoing part of who we
are as persons and as communities. Our individual and shared
experience of being wounded may inform our understanding of
other people's perceptions of their times of desolation, anxiety
or distress, but only if, in processing our hurts, we have found a
new awareness or understanding of ourselves. Pembroke helpfully describes such a deepening of self-awareness – 'It is only
when we have found hope in shadow experiences that we are
able to bring some light through our presence' (2006, 24).

Iona, the pastoral assistant at a local parish church, had been
to John's door to inquire how he was, and John had rather
gruffly and quickly sent her on her way. However, yet again,
John's discerning and caring neighbour, Alice, had mentioned
his increasing withdrawal from, and irritation with his neighbours, at the church door. Iona knew John had leukaemia
and was struggling with coming to terms with his condition. In her gut, Iona felt that he could do with some support.
However, John, normally a friendly and sociable widower
whom Iona knew fairly well, was keeping her and other local
folk at arm's length. What might be a way forward to sensitively offer support to John that was appropriate for him?

Iona took her quandary to her next monthly session with
her pastoral supervisor and together they explored the issue of
withdrawal and isolation and how that might feel. This reso-
nated with Iona's own experience of feeling alone and different from an early age; she was adopted and her adoptive
parents were open about the situation. It occurred to Iona,
with her supervisor's gentle probing, that her own lifelong
struggle with rejection and abandonment as a baby might
offer her some insight into John's situation.

A few days later, after taking some deep breaths, Iona rang
John's doorbell. The door eventually opened and a rather
dishevelled John sighed, 'Iona, listen, I don't want to be rude
but please leave me alone'.

Iona, took another deep breath and said, 'It's hellish feeling alone and being different'.

'How would you know?' retorted John.

'Make me a cup of tea and I'll tell you,' was her reply.

After a pause, came a reluctant nod and the door opened wider. Over tea, Iona briefly shared something of her story and almost before she had finished, John started to cry. Once his sobbing ceased he began to tell his story. Since his initial diagnosis, chemotherapy and the resultant hair loss, lack of appetite and weight loss, some of his family and his best friends from the bowling club were no longer in touch. Even his only son and daughter-in-law who lived in the next town constantly found excuses not to visit. His feelings of rejection and abandonment had led to anger, sadness and huge disappointment. However, paradoxically, at the same time as needing love and attention, John didn't want people to see him, as he felt he had now become a shadow of his former self. He wouldn't want his grandchildren to visit, even if his son had the inclination to bring them. John hated the way he now looked and felt the little ones wouldn't recognize him or would be scared by him. The self-induced part of his isolation was protective – John couldn't bear any more rejection as the result of the fears and anxieties of others.

At the end of an hour's conversation, John had agreed to Iona visiting again in a few days time, as well as contacting his family doctor for an appointment to discuss his low mood, disturbed sleep pattern and lack of appetite. He was also willing for Iona to speak to his neighbour to ask if she would call in and run one or two errands for him as John wasn't keen to leave the house at present.

Iona's own experience of abandonment and feeling different informed the 'empathetic bridge' (Means, 2002, 42) by which she connected with John and established a relationship with him, within which he could tell his story and express himself as he needed to. To seek to do so, Iona had to trust her intuition and have confidence in her sense of self and her level of self-awareness – her wounds had been explored and now integrated into who she had become. Iona offered healing because she had entered the depths of her own experience of feeling alone and isolated and in those depths found wisdom and hope (Campbell, 1986). From experiencing and reflecting on her own interior journey, Iona found the strength and courage to attempt to reach out to John risking further wounding – possible rejection and feelings of failure and helplessness.

Vulnerability and Fear

Sylvia was a divinity student in her thirties who was on placement with Agnes, a chaplain in the local district hospital. She had expressed an interest in hospital chaplaincy with her denomination's central administration and after exploratory conversations they had placed her with Agnes for ten weeks. After an initial introduction to relevant staff and induction to the hospital and her role, Agnes allocated Sylvia three or four wards in which she was to visit patients and follow up referrals from the staff. During the next couple of days, any time Agnes returned to the chaplain's office, she found Sylvia drinking tea and scribbling in a notebook. On enquiring how she was doing, Sylvia would say fine and continue writing. However, at the end of the week, as they started their first supervision session together, Sylvia burst into tears. Gently, when Sylvia was ready, Agnes began to explore what the cause of Sylvia's distress might be. 'It's just too scary. I didn't think it would be as scary as this. Sitting beside ill people, people I'd never met before.'

'Scary,' reflected back Agnes.

'Yes, scary,' repeated Sylvia, 'you just don't know what will come up.'

Sylvia speaks a profound truth in reflecting upon her experience of seeking to provide spiritual or pastoral care. Not one of us ever knows what will emerge out of a caring encounter, for the other or for us as we sit beside them. To attempt to journey with another in a time of illness or uncertainty is to face the unknown and the unpredictable. It is to experience the anxiety and fear in another, and in ourselves.

Scottish practical theologian and writer Kathy Galloway in her poem *Desert 1* which describes Jesus's time in the wilderness, articulates much of what it means to experience vulnerability in the face of the unknown:

> Out beyond the edge of known experience
> lies the desert.
> Were you driven, protesting all the way?
> Were you led, perhaps against your inclination?
> Or did you, curiously, choose a way that culture, church,
> or even better logic would have had you leave alone?
> In the end it didn't matter.
> There you were, across the border,
> over the abyss,
> taking a long
> walk off a short cliff.
> In this scrubby, hostile wilderness,
> there is no shelter, therefore exposure;
> no control, therefore vulnerability;
> and (worst of all) no signposts, therefore confusion.
> Only the stress and strain of hunger
> (no ready-made or obvious source of nourishment,
> and manna is not sweet like honey),
> drought
> (this brackish trickle fills a bitter cup),
> isolation
> (no escape into mirroring others).
> And in the dark, fear.
> And in the fear, darkness,

fearfully anticipating enemies,
and finding you are actually
facing yourself.
It's not so much being shut out from the centre.
In the featureless desert,
where any step in any direction
holds the risk of your being lost,
there are only edges. (1996, 1)

Journeying with others who feel vulnerable, those in a disorientating wilderness experiencing death, loss or ill health is not just a willingness to accompany them into the dark and, often unexplored, interior desert places of their being. It is also to expose ourselves to the similar partially or uncharted territories within us.

Part of the anxiety or fear we might experience when, like Sylvia, we offer to support another in a time of transition or uncertainty, is that we do not know to which places in themselves, and thus potentially within ourselves, another may take us. In offering to support an emotionally or spiritually distressed patient or parishioner, even one with whom we have an established relationship, we take a step into the unknown: their interior unknown and ours. If we, as carers, offer others time and space to open their emotional and spiritual 'internal box', we do not have control of what contents 'come up' or arise out of that box or in what form or order, once the lid has been opened. We can seek to contain and boundary what emerges but our fear of the unknown and what it may ignite in us, may prevent us from establishing therapeutic relationships where people feel safe enough to share, to any degree of depth, their inner selves. Sylvia, during the initial stages of her pastoral placement could not get beyond initial pleasantries with the patients she sought to support. Neither she, nor they, felt confident in her abilities to hold and allow any emerging feelings or issues to be aired, let alone explored, due to her tangible discomfort.

Sylvia has a need to recognize and explore some of her own internal desolate places, with an appropriately trained other, so her inner landscape is more familiar, and thus less threatening, before she can help others to do likewise. Robert Frost highlights the existence of such anxiety provoking inner aspects of our humanity in his poem *Desert Places*:

> Snow falling and night falling fast, oh, fast
> In a field I looked into going past,
> And the ground almost covered in snow,
> But a few weeds and stubble showing last.
>
> The woods around it have it – it is theirs.
> All animals are smothered in their lairs.
> I am too absent-spirited to count;
> The loneliness includes me unawares
>
> And lonely as it is that loneliness
> Will be more lonely ere it will be less –
> A blanker whiteness of benighted snow
> With no expression, nothing to express.
>
> They cannot scare me with their empty spaces
> Between stars – on stars where no human race is.
> I have it in me so much nearer home
> To scare myself with my own desert places.
> (cited by Heaney and Hughes 1981, 125–126)

Not only is our role to create and maintain a safe space in which others may express and explore their lived experience of their desert places. It is also to have some knowledge of our own inner terrain to enable awareness of our countertransference in the face of exposure to dark places in the other which re-open or lay bare our wounds. This may lead us to further explore previously barely charted dark recesses within us with a trusted other and/or withdraw from the care of a particular patient or parishioner and refer them to a suitable colleague.

Vulnerability and spirituality

The spiritual aspect of our human personhood is that element which seeks meaning and purpose in life. Such a dimension is not merely confined to persons of religious faith but is part of what it is to be human. Meaning for any of us may be found in our beliefs and values, expressing and embodying them in worship and daily life. However, meaning is also significantly found in our human relationships, vocational activity, relating to nature and recreational pursuits, the things that make, for each one of us, life worth living or that help us when the chips are down. Elizabeth MacKinlay, an Australian Anglican priest and academic, who has a special interest in spirituality and ageing puts it this way:

> the spiritual element is recognised as that which lies at the core of one's being. I am suggesting that this is a generic concept, in that each person has a spiritual dimension which is worked out in that person's sense of deepest meaning in life. It is from this core of existence, perhaps more properly called the soul, that people respond to life. It is what gets people up in the morning, what they would live or die for; it is what motivates and it is what brings them hope. (2004, 76)

The spiritual dimension within each of us is unique. We all express our spirituality and meet our spiritual needs in different ways. Thus, our spirituality has a significant contribution in shaping our identity – who we are and how we understand ourselves.

There may be times in all our lives when meaning and fulfilment seem elusive or absent, and we question what the point of our life is and who we might really be. Even the core elements that previously had given life purpose and shape may be called into question. Such periods are often linked to tragedy, trauma or a series of wounding events, or they may develop gradually and insidiously, especially in mid- or later life.

The principle character in Blake Morrison's novel *The Last Weekend* is forty-something Ian, who in a rather melancholic mood muses over the challenges of mid-life, including the recognition of the lost and never-to-be-fulfilled hopes and dreams of youth:

> One thing that they don't tell you when you're young, or if they do, you fail to listen, is that getting older doesn't make you any wiser. If life were arranged more fairly, the loss of youth would be offset by knowledge and self-confidence. You would know who you are and where you are going. But, till lately at least, that is not how it has been for me.
>
> The other thing they don't tell you about is depression. Apparently researchers have found that the worst age for depression is forty-four. Not fourteen, when you're a tortured, self-mutilating adolescent. Not seventy-four, when half your friends are dead and you think you're next. But at forty-four; the age I am now, so I read in a recent article, people feel exhausted by their kids (I have none), or suffer the loss of their parents (mine are still going, worst luck), or become aware of their own mortality (I've been aware of mine since I was five). The article makes no mention of what makes people *truly* depressed at forty-four, which is realising that the life they're living is the only one they'll ever have. What hits you at forty-four is that the person you imagined being, and promised yourself you could still become, isn't going to emerge, that you're stuck with who you are till you cease to be. Unless – an even worse prospect – a diminished version of yourself (drunk, drugged, disabled or demented) takes over. (2010, 252)

Midlife is not always met by crisis, by the purchasing of a Harley Davidson, or investing in plastic surgery. However, none of us is immune to such times of acidie, crisis of identity or sense of vocation. No longer being able to find fulfilment and purpose in our working life, or feeling that what we do or embody does not make a difference increases our risk of burnout and reduces our ability to engage in any depth with others (Pines and Aronson, 1988). As Blake Morrison's protagonist reminds us, it is not just in mid-life when spiritual crises are experienced. Adolescents commonly search for meaning in their experience and understanding of the confusing and contradictory world that is unfolding out with (and sometimes within) their family homes, and the elderly may ponder the legacy they will leave behind or the mystery of what awaits them beyond death. At different stages in life, and in different contexts, each of us will have struggled with questions to which there are no easy answers and be left with the scars of our times of most fervent searching. To know the inner map of our spiritual wounding is important, the fact that we, too, may have lacked or are lacking a sense of meaning and purpose in life. Much of what people seek from pastors and chaplains is time and space in which to ask existential questions, to seek to find ways to make life more fulfilling and adjust to altered roles and changes in perceptions of identity. Such spiritual self-knowledge helps prevent us inadvertently projecting our spiritual issues onto others during our encounters with them.

Such times of searching and spiritual disorientation are also, paradoxically, opportunities for personal development. It was no coincidence that Jung felt individuation started in the second half of life! From with a hospice context, Julie Patton describes her understanding of the typical human condition which gives impetus for new growth:

> The shift in psychospiritual energy usually begins when the person feels stagnant or lost. Energy and enthusiasm for customary activities, roles, and commitments begin to wear down. There may also be disillusionment or self-doubt, as the person wonders whether the first half of life was wasted. Contemporary Jungians Janice Brewi and Anne Brennan talk about 'reaching the top of the ladder and finding it is propped up against the

wrong roof.' Physical illness may force recognition of the ultimate fragility of the body. It becomes harder to lose weight or shake off a cold. These realizations usher in a period of turmoil during which the person struggles with issues of meaning and direction. (2006, 305)

Often, it is only getting to the top of the ladder to discover it is leaning against the wrong roof that gives any of us the impetus to seek the help and support we might need to work out which building or roof we are more suited to be aspiring to climb. This can be as true for the pastoral or spiritual carer as it is for the cared for. Intentionally regularly attending to our spiritual lives (exploring that which gives life direction and meaning, including, but not restricted to, our faith) and talking through vocational issues with a spiritual director is crucial in discerning which ladders we choose to climb and learning and growing from the experience if we do find we have opted for the wrong one.

Vulnerability and the ability to care

Each of us carries the scars of significant tears in the tapestry that makes up the story of our lives, which have marked and permanently altered its pattern. Such are the major losses and bereavements that render us vulnerable. Socially, these are the wounds that we and others attend to. The ones which we seek (or others offer) help to process and to attempt to understand – the death of loved ones, serious illness or injury, the end of important relationships or jobs, family leaving home, or moving house and out of supportive communities. However, it is not just major times of transition and adjustment in our personal lives that wound and may limit us, even temporarily, in our ability to care.

Deep-seated wounds in our infancy and childhood can also potentially endanger our capacity to engage meaningfully and therapeutically with those in our care over the long haul. For example, feeding a need for affirmation and worth in life by seeking continual approval from colleagues, patients and parishioners to compensate for deep rooted insecurity and lack of unconditional love in early childhood commonly leads to compassion fatigue and emotional blunting (Taylor, 2007) Such 'masked narcissism' (Grosch and Olsen, 1994) can drive a practitioner to care incessantly until burnout is inevitable, unless the deep source of wounding is understood and worked with.

In our working lives, dealing with traumatic and untimely deaths or losses which have a significant impact on the community in which we work is demanding. These are commonly times of grief and stress which we share with others and are openly talked about and owned. Often in such circumstances, colleagues and congregational members give us permission to grieve also and the time and support in which to do so.

What is more challenging is dealing with the losses and changes that are less commonly publicly acknowledged by us and others, 'disenfranchised grief' (Browning Helsel, 2008). Such unresolved grief includes the accumulated and gradual losses in our professional and private lives which can also threaten our well-being and capacity to empathize and care. For example, the 'ordinary' deaths which pastors, doctors, nurses and other healthcare staff have to deal with on a weekly, if not daily, basis. These may be deaths that are expected, the circumstances not newsworthy; the person not influential and family dynamics reasonably uncomplicated. That is not say that the death of each person does not matter and has no impact. That is the whole point – they do! However, unfortunately, in our busy ecclesial and healthcare cultures there is often little time to process each death, or ending of each relationship with a patient or a relative (when they go home or we go on holiday or if they live a distance away from our parish). As spiritual and pastoral carers, our lives are full of experiencing loss, actual and vicarious; and much of it goes without acknowledgement. We listen to the losses and experience of adjustment of others, we are exposed to their loss of limb or body part, their loss of control, role or identity and what do we do with all of that? Within healthcare, for example, the effect of accumulated loss and exposure to suffering which builds up unnoticed and unprocessed is harmful and dehumanizing unless we intentionally own it and deal with it in a manner that is helpful and restorative for ourselves. In Firth-Cozens and Cornwell's report, *The Point of Care: Enabling Compassionate Care in Acute Hospitals*, they record the experience of a nurse who participated in one of their workshops exploring the issue of compassion in healthcare:

> I went to work on an elderly ward where patients died daily and there was great pressure on beds. At first I did all I could to make the lead up to a death have some meaning and to feel something when one of them died. But gradually the number of deaths and the need to strip down beds and get another patient in as fast as you can get got to me and I became numb to the patients; it became just about the rate of turnover, nothing else. (2009, 6)

Any pastoral or spiritual carer who, for example, performs a significant number of funerals or is regularly involved in supporting others who are suffering or distressed, not just dying or bereaved, may relate to the possibility or actuality of the lived experience this nurse describes.

'The expectation that we can be immersed in suffering and loss daily and not be touched by it is as unrealistic as expecting to be able to walk through water without getting our feet wet' (Remen, 2006, cited in NHS Education for Scotland, 2009, 40). How we as carers sustain and nurture our humanity is an important issue that we shall return to in the final chapter. If we become overloaded with dealing with the wounds of others without sufficient acknowledgement or expression of our inner response to others' loss, any of us can become burnt out. Such overburdening with unprocessed pain and distress may lead to distancing ourselves from any depth of engagement and becoming desensitized to others' emotional and spiritual distress – unconsciously protecting and hiding our vulnerability. Even if our natural propensity is to be empathetic and caring, when suffering from compassion fatigue – especially if our vocation feels as if it has lost its meaning and purpose – any of us, potentially, may not just give less than adequate care, but behave in non-benevolent ways.

Between 2005 and 2009, a series of reviews were carried out at the Mid-Staffordshire NHS Foundation Trust in England because of concerns about mortality rates and the standard of care provided. As a result of these reviews, the Secretary of State for Health set up an inquiry chaired by Robert Francis, Q.C. As part of the inquiry, members of the public shared their experience of the standard and quality of care they received from an overworked and undervalued workforce. The levels of staffing were low and the support and leadership offered to clinical staff was ineffectual, especially in the accident and emergency department and the emergency assessment unit. There was an overwhelming lack of care governance in the healthcare trust. Francis writes of one interview with a relative:

> In one striking case, I was told of the unsympathetic attitude displayed by staff after an elderly patient had tried to take his own life. His relative was present and described how a nurse 'lambasted' him and told him it had been a 'selfish act.' (Department of Health, 2010, 155)

Not only, therefore, do we need a high degree of self-awareness to monitor our energy levels, pastoral capabilities and sense of fulfilment at work, each of us need to be in trusting relationships where not only are we nurtured but challenged if our behaviours and attitudes become unhealthy or potentially harmful (to others and ourselves). We recoil at the depersonalization or development of negative perceptions about patients, linked to burnout (Schaufeli, 1999), by the nurse in Mid-Staffordshire, but stress, disillusionment and lack of support can render us vulnerable to developing a similar lack of compassion and discernment.

Jeffrey Means, an American counsellor and counselling educator, picks up on a spiritual or pastoral carer's need for ongoing, regular emotional and spiritual care and assistance when working with the traumatized or the distressed:

> Working with people toward the goal of transforming destruction and brokenness into healing and wholeness is always difficult, and sometimes terrifying. Doing this with a clear sense of purpose and direction, whilst remaining open and vulnerable to the leading of those with whom we work and the leading of the Spirit, is a difficult balancing act. It demands a great deal from us; and it costs us a lot! In the process we are wounded and forever changed. Only when our eyes remain open to the reality of vicarious traumatization, and only with intentional planning and communal support, will these wounds be as potentially helpful as they are harmful. (2002, 41)

To avoid such harmful wounding for ourselves, the temptation may be to shy away from vulnerability, from engaging with another's pain and, potentially, our own helplessness in the face of their distress and our own. For church workers and chaplains, this may be to play safe and keep uncertainty and existential angst at arms length; to major in task-orientated ministry, focussed on rituals and prayers never staying long enough to get involved in person-centred care which involves waiting with people. Heather and Mark Smith, whose backgrounds are in community education and development, helpfully describe such activity as:

> to focus on technique and on more programmatic approaches. Rather than deal with the untidiness of people's lives and feelings, and to struggle with what might be appropriate responses – we simply take people through some predetermined assessment process and then into a packaged programmes of talk and activity. At a stroke anxiety can be reduced. (2008, 21)

There is a danger also, not unlike the nurse in Mid-Staffordshire relating crudely to a vulnerable patient, that to reduce the risk of exposure to pain and distress we shield ourselves by putting our protective emotional and spiritual armour on, creating an increasingly impenetrable shield of 'getting used to it', 'accepting it comes with the job' and 'not getting too involved' between ourselves and those we seek to care for. The consequence is that it is not just our emotions that become blunted but our humanity, the most significant therapeutic resource any of us possesses, leading not only to the dehumanizing of others but of ourselves.

Christy Kenneally describes in his book *The New Curate* the struggle as a compassionate young clergyman, even in the face of traumatic pastoral situations, not to become numb and hardened in the face of helplessness and great suffering, in order to cope. He writes of anointing an elderly woman whom the cardiac arrest team fail to revive in the hospital where he is Roman Catholic chaplain. His next act is to seek to try to provide some solace to her son, who has been told his mother has died on admission to hospital. All he finds he can do is to rub the bereaved man's back like his father did for him, as he weeps for his mother. Feeling helpless, useless and emotionally wrung out, Kenneally returns to the presbytery where a senior colleague seeks to console him.

He stroked the back of my head with crooked fingers. 'You had a fright, boy; that's all right. Cry away now; sure what are you more than any man? 'Tis something you'll have to get used to.' . . .

How could I tell this saintly soul how much I raged at his disease and his acceptance of it? And how could I face the fear that one day, one awful day, I might 'get used to it'? I might climb into that protective shell where hurts can't come and priests don't cry and it's enough to do what must be done. And who would I be then? (1997, 36)

Remaining Vulnerable and Open

Finding ways for ourselves as carers to be able to sustain our humanity and ability to be vulnerable with others over time is crucial for our personal well-being and vocational fulfil-ment as much as it is for the quality of the care we provide. We need to find and maintain the balance between becom-ing swamped and overwhelmed by the wounds of others and distancing ourselves from them. In addition, we need to find a way to process what impact the caring relationships that we are involved in have on ourselves. New York-based clinical psychologist Yael Danieli (2006, 264–5) offers some strategies to what she terms 'self-healing':[1]

1. Recognise our reactions:

   - What are the signs and signals that indicate we are stressed, for example, altered sleeping pattern, irritability, difficulty concentrating?
   - Find words or images to describe our thoughts and feel-ings. 'What cannot be talked about (or drawn or sculpted or musically played?)[2] can also not be put to rest; and if it

---

1   The fourth point is an addition to Danieli's original schema.
2   The words in parenthesis are mine.

is not, the wounds continue to fester from generation to generation.' (Bettelheim, 1984, 166)

2. Contain our reactions:

- Identifying our personal level of tolerance to hearing *anything* – how much and to what depth of any particular subject can we listen to reasonably comfortably whilst being open and receptive to what is being said. For example, power in abusive relationships or feelings of abandonment and lack of security. Danieli, helpfully, reminds us that every feeling 'has a beginning, a middle and an end' so that if we are afraid of being overwhelmed by its intensity we can reduce our fear by learning to track it from its start to its finish. Thus, seeking to let it be without defensive counter-transference measures (see Chapter 5).

3. Heal and grow through:

- Seeking to accept nothing ever stays or will be the same.
- If we feel overwhelmed, burnt out or as if we are not coping – we need to take time to acknowledge and deal with what is problematic by seeking appropriate help and working through what arises. This requires taking time away from work and not returning until others, as well as ourselves, feel we are ready.
- Seeking support to deal with wounds re-opened or previously un-recognised through interacting with patients and parishioners' stories.
- Developing a network of people with whom we can wrestle with issues of death, dying, suffering and theodicy.
- Having a varied range of creative and playful interests through which we can express ourselves and truly be ourselves outside work.

4. Nurturing a theology of self

Ongoing engagement with a theology of self, who we are in relation to God, as well as a theology of our vocation is significant. Reminding ourselves that we are beloved of God – a child of God whom God loves and wants the best for is important. In addition, remembering that though seeking to embody God's love, none of us is God, helps to keep our role and our significance in perspective.

Vulnerability and Love

Like St Julian and young Christy Kenneally, much of our motivation for caring for others may be love. However, following Christ in loving the vulnerable – the sick, the outcast and the stranger – and attempting to replicate the manner in which he loved, is dangerous, as Sydney Carter's poem *Mother Teresa* reminds us:

> No revolution will come in time
> to alter this man's life
> except the one
> surprise of being loved.
>
> It is too late to talk of Civil Rights,
> neo-Marxism,
> psychiatry
> or any kind of sex.
>
> He has only twelve more hours to live.
> Forget about
> a cure for cancer, smoking, leprosy
> or osteo-arthritis.
>
> Over this dead loss to society
> you pour your precious ointment,
> wash the feet
> that will not walk tomorrow.
>
> Mother Teresa, Mary Magdalene,
> your love is dangerous, your levity
> would contradict
> our local gravity.

But if love cannot do it, then I see
no future for this dying man or me.
So blow the world to glory,
crack the clock. Let love be dangerous. (2000,
82–3)

Such loving is dangerous – it unsettles and disturbs. Sometimes it is the loved, perhaps experiencing compassion for the first time who are perturbed; often it is those who observe who are challenged and their status quo ruffled. The Scribes and Pharisees certainly were by Jesus loving the rejected and the ritually unclean and by the way in which he did so. Unconditional, compassionate loving is also hazardous for the carer. In giving we may indeed receive – fulfilment, meaning, new understanding or the challenge of a different perspective or theological questions to ponder. Yet, in loving we risk – rejection, failure and disappointment. In loving, we are drained and diminished, rendered vulnerable. Unconditional loving, *agape*, wounds us. It is costly, as Means and Keneally remind us. So much so, that, unchecked or unlimited, it can destroy us. The next chapter explores the necessary limiting of our loving and the intentional making of ourselves vulnerable.

7
Limited Self

Terry put down the phone and sighed. His colleague Jess, who shared an office with him, turned to see Terry with his head in his hands. 'It's labour suite, another baby.' Terry sighed again as he looked up. 'I don't think I can do it. . . .' He paused to sigh again.

'I'll go if you want,' interjected Jess, 'I know how full your diary is.' Terry shook his head. There were now tears running down his face. 'No, I don't think I can do it anymore . . . this job.'

Terry was three years into his first chaplaincy job in a large teaching hospital. He was part of a team of three full-time chaplains (the lead Grace, Jess and Terry), Harry – a part-time chaplain, Jenny – a half-time secretary, and a small team of chaplaincy volunteers. Terry's diary was always full but, even then, nobody ever knew where he was and what he was doing in the hospital – it was a bone of contention in the team. Terry never said no to anything and was usually last out of the office at night. He was a warm and kind spiritual carer, his company enjoyed by his colleagues and his support appreciated by hospital staff and patients alike. However, lately he had become a bit tetchy and less communicative. He always seemed tired and recently had double-booked himself for a couple of appointments as well as forgetting a pre-funeral visit he had arranged to do. One or two staff had mentioned to Grace that they hadn't see Terry on their wards recently – wards which he covered. In turn, Grace had intentionally asked Terry a couple of months ago how he was and he had said he was feeling a bit off colour but nothing more.

Just then Grace came into the room and quickly grasped the situation. 'Come on, Terry, I'll take you home. Jess will take the call and hold your pager.' Terry went home with Grace that afternoon and did not return to work for five months. He not only required the support of his general practitioner but that of a counsellor and of his friends, family and local faith community. He had become emotionally, spiritually and physically exhausted and socially isolated.

To deepen our awareness of ourselves and how we relate others is a significant factor in enabling the enhancement of our well-being as well as those we seek to care for. Alison Webster, a Social Responsibility Advisor in the Church of England, outlines what well-being may be:

> It [human well-being] has to do with the interweaving of the psychological, the physical and the spiritual; it includes an element of how we inhabit our personal histories and how we negotiate these in our present; it depends upon our inter-relationship with others – relationships which offer the possibility of harm and of flourishing – and, finally, it involves questions of identity. Wellbeing must be about naming oneself, not being named by others; naming our limitations as we understand them, not as others do. And living with them, while also extending ourselves in ways that do not undermine our naming. (2002, 22)

The aim of this short chapter is to help the readers to raise awareness of their limitations, even to name some. This is intended to be perceived as a positive exercise, not as a means of chastizing or browbeating, in helping practitioners accept limitation as part of our humanity and to frame and prioritize our caring activity.

'Being alive is about embracing our humanity, our flesh, our boundedness and our unboundedness' (Woodward 2005, 74). Understanding our personhood is not just about deepening our awareness of who we are and how we relate to others, it is also about developing an understanding of our limitations. This includes what we are not so good at or cannot offer, at that particular moment or in the longer term, to the benefit of others or ourselves. None of us can be on the top of our 'pastoral game' every hour of every day. We can only offer others what we can, when we can. More than that, we can only be who we are as caregivers. There is no formulaic model for delivering spiritual or pastoral care, no ideal carer we should aspire to be. We can only become more aware of who we really are, including accepting our limitations, enabling us to be more of an authentic presence with others rather than seeking to be something we are not. As Nouwen points out, 'The first responsibility of the pastor is to help his parishioner become aware of the kind of help he really wants and to let him know if he is able to give it to him' (1978, 54). In addition, it also important to realize that we must limit what we offer or give to others and that it is permissible, indeed imperative, to do so. We need to keep some of our energy, our time, our compassion and our love for ourselves, our family and our friends.

Limitations to Our Role and Abilities

Terry worked in a team, not just with other chaplains but with those from other healthcare disciplines. As part of his staggered return to work, Grace, as his line manager, arranged a series of planned meetings with Terry to see if they could identify potential sources of stress for Terry at work. During these conversations, they explored how they might deal with these and develop sensible limits to Terry's workload. During these encounters, it transpired that Terry struggled to define what his role was, not just in relation to the other healthcare professions he worked with, in different units and wards, but also within the chaplaincy team.

Terry had worked for many years as a parish priest within the Anglican tradition in a rural parish. He had, on the whole, done so as a single practitioner, with the support of his parish council. As a chaplain, Terry had a job description and he had tried hard to fulfil his obligations to his employer, the local healthcare trust. However, he found the job outline rather vague and even his annual appraisals hadn't really helped him to work out what his priorities as a hospital chaplain really were. Terry knew it was about supporting patients, their carers and hospital staff, but it was obvious he, and the chaplaincy team as a whole, couldn't see everyone. In addition, he wasn't sure if the chaplaincy team had a clear understanding of their remit and wondered why there was no such thing as a development or strategic plan for their department. Grace found this uncomfortable to hear but was open enough to take Terry's comments on board. Hence, together with Jess and Harry, they made plans to develop a statement clarifying chaplaincy's unique role in the hospital and to make agreed work priorities and work plans. The four of them, as well as Jenny, the department secretary, also took a day out of the hospital, facilitated by a chaplain from a neighbouring trust, to consider their own and each others' gifts and natural abilities. They talked about how they could encourage best use of each others' gifts and how they might support each others in their limitations. As a result of this, it was agreed that Terry would develop the department's educational programme to facilitate the teaching of spiritual care to pre- and post-registration healthcare practitioners from a variety of disciplines. He had experience in developing adult education classes within the diocese where he had previously worked and Grace had received some really positive feedback from the hospital's education department when Terry had done some work with them the year before. It was also decided that Jenny would manage Terry's diary and that at weekly meetings the team, from now on, would intentionally discuss and plan together forthcoming activities and priorities.

Firth-Cozens and Cornwell outline characteristics of a good team working in healthcare which have significance for any group of colleagues seeking to work together to provide care and support for others:

- The task is defined and its objectives clear.
- It has reasonably clear boundaries and is not too large (ideally fewer than 10 people).
- The membership know who leads it and the leadership is good.
- There is participation in decision-making by all members, good communication, and frequent interaction between them.
- It meets regularly to review its objectives, methods and effectiveness.
- Its meetings are well conducted.
- Its members trust each other and feel safe to speak their minds.
- There is a shared commitment to excellence of care. (2009, 7)

In relation to Firth-Cozens and Cornwell's traits of a well functioning team, Terry's burnout and his team's response to it were providing a catalyst for team-building and, thus, reducing stress for its members in the long run (Carter and West, 1999).[1] It is vital to have clarity of our vocational role and understand the expectations of our employer and colleagues as to how they feel our role might be carried out in the particular context we are working in. This involves not only having a job description, but seeking to marry our perceptions of our role and its responsibilities with that of those we work with and for. Moreover, when working in a team setting, it is crucial to be aware of the roles of others and the boundaries between members' roles. Communication regarding roles and

---

1   Carter and West (1999) report that members of good teams have lower stress levels.

responsibilities within a team setting is important, as is mutual respect for the negotiated or given limitations of each person's role. Without such explicitly agreed boundaries, uncertainty and tension may develop within a team, potentially effecting individual and corporate well-being and morale.

As a result of Terry's conversations with Grace, Jenny made appointments for him with several key members of the multi-disciplinary healthcare and administrative team he worked with to find out more about their roles. This was especially necessary to help Terry work more collaboratively with those who also supported bereaved parents and relatives. It transpired that, previously, he had spent much time and energy helping parents whose babies were stillborn or had died *in utero*, dealing with legal and administrative issues. By meeting with the hospital's bereavement officer and hearing about her role, Terry understood more clearly the boundaries of his role and when he should refer to her parents who were struggling to cope with legislative and practical issues. A conversation with one of the hospital social workers enabled a deeper understanding of the local services available for those with housing problems and when Terry might refer patients or their carers to social work services.

Being aware of the limitations of our role and our abilities not only helps us to focus our time and energy on what we are paid or are expected by others to do. It also gives us permission to spend our time concentrating on what we are gifted or good at (that assumes we are in a role which affords us that opportunity), without worrying about more peripheral issues. Invariably, performing a role which enables us to focus on utilizing our strengths and gifts leads to enhanced vocational fulfilment.

Referring service users or parishioners to other services or colleagues is not to fail. It is to recognize either a person's need is beyond our giftedness or competency or that their need would be better met by someone else at that particular moment in time. Robin Green (1987), an English Anglican pastoral theologian, insightfully suggests humility is an important trait for worship leaders to possess. It is also a significant quality for the spiritual or pastoral carer to own. For a ministry team in an ecclesial context or a healthcare multidisciplinary or chaplaincy team to embody and enact humility, it requires a shared non-competitive ethos and motivation to care for each other. In addition, it calls for an enjoyment and admiration of our own and each other's abilities.

To be aware of our professional and personal limitations is a great strength. It is not only pastorally and morally best practice but significant in preserving the wellbeing of the carer.

Limiting Our Vocational Giving

Terry had left his previous job as a parish priest shortly after his marriage had ended. He had always enjoyed pastoral work and threw himself into hospital chaplaincy. His evenings and weekends were long and lacked pleasure or purpose, apart from when his teenage daughter came to visit. He often found it easier to stay later working in the hospital, there was always another patient to visit or staff member who was keen to offload, than to go home to an empty flat. Terry's motivation for pastoral martyrdom was as much to fill the void in his life with busyness, than simply responding to spiritual needs of others.

Jesuit Father Laforgue, the central character in Brian Moore's (1987) novel *Black Robe,* discovered through his developing relationships with, and understanding of, indigenous Algonkian tribespeople in seventeenth century North America that his role was not to convert such 'heathen savages' but to live with them and love them. His understanding of his Jesuit calling was to give himself completely to this task and to be unflinching and unfailing in such giving of himself, even if this meant his life itself.

Pastorally or spiritually, this is not the way of Jesus. He loved, felt compassion, reached out to and wept with, and for, others. However, Jesus' love was boundaried – he did not give all of his self to everyone all of the time during his short ministry (a ministry not much longer than Terry's chaplaincy). Even amongst the crowds, Jesus only reached out to specific individuals.[2] Jesus also intentionally drew a line to how much he could give. At times, he withdrew from people, in all their neediness and with all their expectations of him.[3] He took time apart to prioritize his own restoration and spiritual nurturing – time to be alone with God, time to relax in the company of friends, to enjoy conversation and food and drink. Jesus was open to enjoy receiving the time, love, hospitality and the generosity of others without feeling guilty. In addition, Jesus didn't always respond immediately to the needs of others; sometimes he discerned it was appropriate to wait before intervening. Neither did he attempt to meet the needs of those seeking his help all at one time; Jesus prioritized (Litchfield, 2006).[4]

In the end, Jesus was crucified – who he loved and cared for, what he taught and raised questions about was too uncomfortable for those in power. Yet he did not crucify himself with overwork and endless giving. Not for Jesus total immersion in the endless needs, actual or imagined, of the ill, the insane, the desperate and the dying.

We have to ask ourselves whose need is being met if we are tempted to drown ourselves in a sea of unending giving.

---

2 For example, Matthew 8: 1–4 – a passage in which Jesus is followed by 'great crowds' down a mountain. He responds to pleas of one man amongst many, a leper, to heal him. In Luke 19: 1–10 – Jesus reaches out to the ostracised Zacchaeus, a tax collector, who climbs a tree to see Jesus over the crowds.

3 In Mark 1: 35, Jesus takes time alone to pray.

4 In John 11: 1–6, Jesus waits before he visits Lazarus, after his sisters had informed Jesus of his illness. In Mark 1: 29–31, however, Jesus responds quickly to the needs of Simon's sick mother-in-law. In Mark 5: 21–43, he chooses first to relate to the woman with excessive menstrual bleeding before responding to the needs of Jarius, the leader of the synagogue, who had approached him beforehand.

Terry, in his need to avoid the pain of bereavement and the emptiness in his private life, sought to meet his needs in seemingly responding to those of others. Pastoral ministry is attractive to those who have unmet spiritual needs. Meaning, purpose and fulfilment lacking in other aspects of our lives can be compensated for in our vocational work. There will always be those in hospitals or parishes, in churches or prisons, who will be content to receive a visit and the danger is we end up like Terry, emotionally and spiritually drained. We may well have caring family, friends or colleagues who warn us of over commitment. However, unless we are aware of our own needs and internal drivers and set boundaries to our caring and self-giving, there will always be the possibility of the waves of compassion fatigue crashing over our heads. In short, as pastoral and spiritual care givers, we need to take responsibility for our own well-being and, as Webster and Woodward suggest, own and respect our human limitations. Christ calls us to love the naked, the hungry, the vulnerable, and the sick but not to crucify ourselves in doing so. Terry's lack of ability to leave the hospital at night not only points to a deep spiritual need (a lack of meaning and purpose outwith his working life), but an urgent need for theological reflection on his practice. Jesus calls us to be his people, to be ourselves and utilize the gifts we have been given to embody his compassion and care in doing so. Importantly, however, we are not called to be Christ. For many of us who steep ourselves in delivering spiritual and pastoral care, like Terry we need to remember the role of Messiah has already been taken! (Muse 2000).

Crucially we must also realize that other people's healing and journey towards wholeness depends on their motivation and attitude and not just our care. Jesus offered healing and new opportunities in life for the sick, the lame and the outcast, but they had to respond to his reaching out in order to be healed.[5] Elizabeth Taylor, an American nurse with a particular interest in spiritual care, points out that as carers we have to limit the amount of ourselves we can give to others and allow them to take ultimate responsibility for their own well-being:

> the goal for healers is . . . to understand the patient compassionately. Such compassion involves respecting patients' choices and ways of processing suffering; it does not involve controlling or manipulating the attitudes or solutions chosen by patients. Compassionate HCPs (healthcare professionals), therefore, are kept from burning out because they understand the limits of their responsibility and do not over-own patients' outcomes. (2007, 14),

We can offer as much as realistically we can to others in terms of our time, energy and compassion, the rest is up to them. As for us, when we leave 'the Helper' fills the space we leave behind.[6] Handing patients or parishioners over to the care of the Holy Spirit when we leave them or at the end of a day's work not only reminds us of our limitations and need to let go. It makes us mindful that ultimately someone greater holds them, as well as us, in their care.

5　John 5: 2–18 tells the story of the man who had been ill for thirty eight years and lay by the pool near Jerusalem's Sheep Gate, waiting for someone to help him into the water deemed to have healing properties. Jesus puts the onus firmly on the crippled man to decide if he has the will and determination to cast off his sick role. 'Do you want to be made well?' Jesus asks him. Only when the man indicates that he has the desire to bath in the pool does Jesus respond.

6　In John 16: 7, Jesus, after he washes his disciples' feet in the upper room, says to them, 'Nevertheless, I tell you the truth; it is to your advantage that I go away, for if I do not go away, the Advocate (or the Helper) will not come to you; but if I go I will send him to you'. For a fuller exploration of the importance of respectful absence as a part of spiritual and pastoral care provision, see Kelly (2007, 92–94) and Nouwen (1977).

Remembering that we are limited, and having an awareness of what our particular as well as our shared human limitations are, is just as significant for delivering sensitive spiritual and pastoral care as being aware of our gifts and abilities.

Chapter 8 will help the reader to engage with the ultimate human limitation – our mortality.

8

Mortal Self

The days of our life are seventy years, or perhaps eighty if we are strong; even then their span is only toil and trouble; they are soon gone, and we fly away.[1]

Our mortality is a universal facet of our human existence, a given dimension of our personhood. Death is an absolute certainty – we cannot avoid it. However, in the Western world, we spend much of our time and energy seeking to deny or defy this fact. Yet, Nature, if we attend to her, has a way of reminding us of our fragility and transient existence. At different times in our lives, we become more aware of our physical limitations – when the stairs begin to steepen, familiar distances to be walked lengthen and the time taken to do so increases – as well as our reducing mental agility and the lessening capacity of our organs to work as they once did. For the majority of us, such insights are increasingly discovered in our middle and later years of life. As a result, our habits and behaviours are forced to change to accommodate altered functioning, and an awareness of our ageing and death heightens. The American poet Allen Ginsberg knowingly and playfully captures the ageing process, embraced or not, in his poem *These knowing age*:

> These knowing age
> fart
> These knowing age
> walk slowly

---

1 Psalm 90: 10.

124

these knowing age
remind themselves of their grandmothers
these knowing age
take waterpills, high blood pressure,
watch their sugar and salt
these knowing age eat less meat, some
stopped smoking a decade ago
Some quit coffee, some drink it strong.
These knowing age saw
best friends' funerals, telephoned
daughters and granddaughters.
Some drive, some don't, some cook, some
do not.
These knowing age often
keep quiet. (1999, 8)

Ageing corresponds with physical changes creeping up on us – aches and pains becoming noticeable, waistlines expanding, our hair greying, our capacity for exercise reducing and muscle tone slackening. For men, receding hairlines, more frequent visits to the bathroom and, perhaps, lessening virility are reminders of physical ageing. Women have to live through symptoms of the menopause and an end to fertility. The potential change in our shape, looks, bodily functions, interest in sex and ability to reproduce influences not only the way we feel about ourselves but our whole identity – as does being offered regular health checks for various cancers, high blood pressure and diabetes, as well as the increased likelihood of us, and our peers, being diagnosed and living with a chronic physical or cognitive disorder which cannot be cured. Many of the population in the Western world, in middle or advanced years live with one or more medical conditions which, though alleviated and perhaps their advancement slowed, serve as a reminder of our ageing and mortality. In midlife, we begin to realize that more than half our lifespan may have past. Therefore, we may not only begin to consider our death but also our life's purpose, what we have done and what we want to do with our remaining years. Our fear may be that life has passed us by, that life is running away from us or that we may develop physical disease or dementia that renders us helpless, hopeless and a burden on others. It is tempting to deny such threats and challenges to our lives by deflecting our attention from them in our busyness and frenetic activity as we seek material security, kudos and status in the communities and organizations we inhabit and work in. However, such experience of ageing and the anticipation of death, is part of life. To what extent we acknowledge, process and incorporate these elements of human experience into our personhood influences not only our approach to life but also our quality of relating:

In the midst of life we be in death.

These words from the 1559 edition of *The Book of Common Prayer* (Booty 1976, 309) relate a simple yet profound truth – death is an integral part of life. As we are living, so we are dying and as we are dying we are also still living. Estonian poet Jaan Kaplinski puts it this way:

Death does not come from outside. Death is within.
Born – grows together with us. (2002, 375)

This chapter seeks to help the reader to reflect on their mortality and the significance of awareness that death is, indeed, part of each of our lives. The underlying premise of this chapter is the belief that it is not possible to sensitively accompany another on their journey towards death, if we have not yet intentionally begun to consider our own. In developing a heightened awareness of our personal attitudes to our mortality, we are more able to appreciate and make a safe space available for others to explore theirs. If we are not engaging with, and acknowledging in an ongoing manner, our own feelings and beliefs about death how can we separate out our perspectives, anxieties and fears from another's? Philip Browning Hensel of Princeton Theological Seminary writes:

> ministry is often grief work, . . . a grief associated with losing those whom the pastor has known and cared for through her ministry and the challenges associated with liminality. As a person who is associated with death, the pastor feels both the social marginalization that comes from this position, and also the challenging personal experience of facing loss. The minister finds it necessary both to grieve the loss of persons whom she has come to love and admire, as well as work through the inevitable reality of her own mortality. (2009, 7)

Doing our own grief work is a challenging and nuanced, yet necessary, business if we are to be an effective therapeutic resource to the dying and bereaved. We may never completely accept our mortality or be entirely comfortable with the fact that our time on earth is limited, but being prepared to explore our attitudes, beliefs and feelings about death and dying may give us some empathy regarding the concerns and fears of others. Unless, we find ways of doing our grief work in an ongoing intentional way then we will eventually become overloaded with loss and struggle to relate to others with any depth or meaning, both in our professional and personal lives. One approach to doing so is creatively developing or utilising appropriate rituals. For example, in the hospice where I worked, short times of ritual remembering every six weeks or so were established, to which bereaved family members and friends of those who had died in the hospice were invited. During these times of remembrance, those attending had the opportunity to light a candle to acknowledge the significance of their deceased loved one. Over the months, an increasing number of members of staff, including myself, began to participate in this ritual action. It became our way of acknowledging our loss and grieving in relation to the numerous patients that we had cared for who had died. More than that, we as staff, were consciously or sub-consciously, marking the lost relationships with them and their carers, and all the love and meaning we had invested.

In our contemporary world, the emotional and physical energy and finance which we invest in keeping the spectre of ageing and death off our lips and out of sight and mind is proportionate to the depth of vulnerability we feel in its constant shadow. For example, in England and Wales, less than 20 per cent of the population die at home (Gomes and Higginson, 2008), and it is predicted that by 2030 less than one in ten of the British population will do so. The vast majority die a more sanitized and distant death in hospitals, care homes and hospices.

Euphemisms for death and dying are not only heard and read in the media but are all too often commonly articulated in everyday conversations in the English speaking world. How often do we hear the phrases 'passed away', 'passed on', 'we lost her', 'gone to a better place' or 'slept away'? That death and its consequences cannot be openly named by individuals, families and communities, including in churches and healthcare facilities, is an indicator of its perceived threat and our unspoken vulnerability and fear.

Even in a Western world where improved palliative care has helped the development of more holistic end of life healthcare, death is still viewed as failure by many healthcare professionals. Death is still perceived as a medical problem to be conquered, 'resisted, postponed or avoided' (Clark, 2002, 905), rather than an inevitable part of life to be accepted when further treatment is inappropriate, impossible or unwanted.

If we were more able to talk about death and bereavement when we are well and our loved ones are healthy, perhaps we may be more equipped to deal with its reality when death and bereavement become a lived experience in our family and personal story.

Arguably, life would have little meaning without our knowledge and experience of inevitable loss, death and bereavement. But while in some ways our society is obsessed with death – with reports of violent, sudden and unexpected death paraded across our media every day – it is still very difficult to talk about this one shared certainty in terms that relate to our own deaths or those of people close to us. (Seymour et al., 2010, 646)

This was not so for the ancient Hebrews. Mortality was a fact of life and 'not something to be regretted or challenged' (Davidson, 1983, 28). The wisdom of Psalm 49, for example, is very matter-of-fact about death being a part of the life of all, no matter our station or status.

> When we look at the wise, they die;
> fool and dolt perish together
> and leave their wealth to others.
> Their graves are their homes forever,
> their dwelling places to all generations,
> though they named lands their own.
> Mortals cannot abide in their pomp;
> they are like the animals that perish.[2]

God breathed life into humanity and, at the end, men and women return to the earth from which their mortal frame was fashioned.[3] The New English Bible in its translation of Ecclesiastes 3: 19–20 is very clear in making this point:

For man is a creature of chance, and the beasts are creatures of chance, and one mischance awaits them all: death comes to all alike. They all draw the same breath. Men

---

2 Psalm 49: 10–12.
3 See Genesis 2–3, for example, Genesis 3: 19: 'By the sweat of your face you shall eat bread until you return to the ground, for out of it you were taken; you are dust, and to dust you shall return.'

have no advantage over the beasts. All go to the same place: all came from the dust, and to the dust all return.

Old Testament scholars and pastoral theologians alike mourn the institutional collusion involved in the notable exclusion of the psalms of lament from contemporary worship, despite their healing potential to help us articulate and explore our human perplexity and pain in the face of suffering and death.[4] In doing so, we deny ourselves a significant part of our Judeo-Christian heritage and the symbolic integration of loss, death and suffering as part of liturgy and life.[5] Such an omission not only buffers us from the fact that there is much in life that is beyond our control and that God may not be the God we want God to be – one who ensures our lives are full of order and well-being if we are faithful (Swinton, 2007). It also prevents us having to regularly confront our human limitations, especially our mortality and that of those we love. Such psalms are hard to hear but they speak of realities experienced and shared since the beginning of human existence – they are the very stuff of helping humanity to normalize the existence and expression of intense fears and unanswerable questions in the face of ill-fortune, illness and death. For example, Psalm 22 articulates poignantly the human lot of dealing with the pain and loneliness of anticipated death:

> My God, my God, why have you
> forsaken me.
> Why are you so far from helping me,
> from the words of my groaning?
> O my God, I cry by day, but you do not

---

4 In relation to Old Testament studies, see, for example, Robert Davidson (1983) and Walter Brueggemann (1984). In relation to pastoral and practical theology, see Stanley Hauwerwas (1990), Denise Ackermann (1998) and John Swinton (2007).

5 Robert Davidson (1983) points out that there are more psalms of personal lament in the Old Testament than any other form of psalm.

answer;
and by night, but find no rest.

I am poured out like water,
and all my bones are out of joint;
my heart is like wax;
it is melted away within my breast;
my mouth is dried up like a potsherd,
and my tongue sticks to my jaws;
you lay me in the dust of death.[6]

Yet no matter how much, as death denying or defying communities and individuals in the Western world, we try to sideline or keep death at arms length, death is very much around:

it is always with us, scratching at some inner door, whirring softly, barely audible, just under the membrane of consciousness. Hidden and disguized, leaking out in a variety of symptoms, it is the wellspring of many of our worries, stresses, and conflicts. (Yalom, 2008, 9)

Fear of Death and Dying

In the twenty-first century, the average length of life may have lengthened in the affluent Western world yet what has not changed since ancient times is the sense of vulnerability mortality invokes in human beings. Shakespeare (cited in Heaney and Hughes, 1981, 55), though typically lyrical, poignantly encapsulates humanity's universal fear of death, in 'Aye, but to die, and go we know not where' from *Measure for Measure*:

Aye, but to die, and go we know not where;
To lie in cold obstruction and to rot;

---

6   Psalm 22: 1–2 and 14–15.

This sensible warm notion to become
A kneaded clod; and the delighted spirit
To bathe in fiery floods, or to reside
In thrilling region of thick-ribbed ice;
To be imprison'd in the viewless winds,
And blown with restless violence round about
The pendant world; or to be worse than worst
Of those that lawless and incertain thoughts
Imagine howling: 'tis too horrible!
The weariest and most loathed worldly life
That age, ache, penury and imprisonment
Can lay on nature is a paradise
To what we fear of death. (Act 3, Scene 1)

To fear death is a normal human response. There are many reasons why our earthly demise may fill us with dread. The process of dying itself fills many with dread – fear of pain, losing control, drowning in one's own bronchial or upper respiratory secretions, fatal haemorrhaging or being alone are common in those whose illness has become incurable. For patients receiving palliative care, being able to talk openly about what pharmacological, spiritual, emotional and social support is available during the terminal phase of their illness may be very important. Some patients may also want to know what will be the most probable cause of their actual death for people with their condition and what commonly happens during the process of death. This may help reduce this aspect of their fear of the unknown. Psychotherapist Irvin Yalom helpfully expands on the theme of dying as a journey we have to go on our own, no matter what our beliefs around the existence of an afterlife and what form it may take:

Dying . . . is lonely, the loneliest event of life. Dying not only separates you from others but also exposes you to a second, even more frightening form of loneliness: separation from the world itself. (2008, 119)

Jesus cry of dereliction on the cross was of a man who truly felt alone as he approached death; even the Godhead is felt to abandon him at the last.[7]

Death is final. It is separates us from the security and love of our family and friends as well as the physical and emotional pleasure of living and the meaning and purpose in our lives. Andrew Grieg puts it this way:

> Awoken to my physical being. Body is my ground, my reality, my sanity. I love and trust its appetites, its movement, the five senses that like eager messengers bring the world to me. I'll never entirely adjust to its inevitable demise. I can almost accept it, but by God I regret it. When life, physical life is so good – how can I not hate leaving it. (2006a, 132)

James Woodward, an English pastoral theologian with a close interest in spirituality and ageing, echoes Grieg's sentiment; 'Death is about learning how to give up what we have embodied' (2005, 74). Both Woodward and Grieg refer to death as a leaving behind the physical, and, thus, the sensual and relational aspects of being human. Being mortal is to have the gift of being able to enjoy our bodies and how we relate to our physicality, to other beings and the living world around us. Yet, it is also to realize that losing these potential sources of pleasure is a universal human experience.

Death comes and we cannot control its timing or its effect. It renders a tear in the lives of those we leave behind, ripping asunder the pattern of shared plans, hopes and aspirations. For the most part, death is treated as an unspoken spectre which lurks in the shadows and, because of this,

---

7   Mark 15: 34 – At three o'clock Jesus cried out with a loud voice, '*Eloi, Eloi, lema sabachthani?*' which means 'My God, my God, why have you forsaken me?'

renders us all the more vulnerable. Whatever we believe happens after death and to whom, is not a matter of fact. As the bard alludes to, part of our fear of death is our fear of not knowing – no one can say with any certainty what happens after the terminal event to the essence of our being. Rowan Williams further reflects on the impact of this in his poem, *Experiencing Death (Rilke)*:

> Don't know a thing about this trip we're going on; they don't
>
> give much away about it. So we don't know where to stand
>
> to look at the unwelcome destination, how to see our death.
>
> Amazed? entranced? or loathing? How the tragic mask twists things. (2002a, 79)

It is, therefore, of great importance that we as pastoral and spiritual carers have at least begun to explore our vulner-abilities, fears and beliefs in relation to our mortality and the process of dying. If we don't have some awareness of the anxieties we carry about our own mortality in our inner recesses, and some understanding of the cause of them, then the space we seek to make for others to explore theirs will inevitably restrict the depth and openness of sharing. Our attitudes and feelings will be greatly shaped by early experi-ences and familial, ecclesial and community enculturation. In addition, our personal and professional encounters with ill-health and death and our degree of reflection on them will also be significant. Ongoing and intentional reflec-tion on practice affords us the opportunity to explore and revisit our attitudes, vulnerabilities and theological ques-tions around death, dying and suffering. This not only offers possibilities to inform our future practice but to live our personal lives more fully.

The Benefits of Contemplating Our Mortality

'We derive meaning not only by working and loving, but also from the art of dying. We learn about ourselves through the life and death of others.' (Streets, 1996, 183)

Andrew was a 71-year-old man dying from lung cancer, whom the respiratory ward sister had asked me, as a hospital chaplain, to see. He was desperate to get home to be with his wife, Jeanie, and a package of care was already in place for him to do so. However, due to Andrew's current level of agitation, the ward staff were not willing to discharge him at present. Indeed, they were contemplating increasing his medication to make him more relaxed and, thus, drowsy, if not sleepy. On introducing myself, Andrew was quick to point out that he was not a churchgoer nor religious. However, he was happy to talk once he established I wasn't selling either!

Andrew was born and bred in Glasgow and was very proud of his Marxist upbringing. His parents had sent him to a socialist Sunday School whilst all his friends went to the kirk on a Sunday morning. All his life he had fought for justice for the working man and woman in the trade union movement, his values base being formed not through faith and worship but political rhetoric and rallies.

Andrew knew he was dying and, though he wanted to spend his remaining days at home with Jeanie, paradoxically, what also gave him hope was the thought that death was imminent. He explained that all his life he had been in control and had found meaning in leading campaigns, encouraging and supporting others, and being the bread winner and head of the household. Now everything in his life was out of his control and others were in the driving seat – the cancer was in charge and now answered to no one, the doctors and nurses dictated his medication and care and now his coming and goings. Andrew felt helpless, useless and a burden to Jeanie, his family and the state. He had never believed in God but was God now having the last laugh – showing him who really was in control! For Andrew, death would bring an end to his helplessness, or at least allow him not to have anything or anybody else in control. After death there was nothing – no cancer, no healthcare professionals, no mind-deadening drugs and no God.

My role was to listen to Andrew's story – to hear how he had made his mark and found meaning and purpose in life. It was to allow him to express his anxiety and vulnerability regarding the experience of living with, and dying from, cancer. In the sacred space we negotiated together, Andrew found hope as he told someone for the first time his paradoxical spiritual and social needs as well as feeling comfortable enough to utter, hitherto unthinkable thoughts, that theodicy was something he was struggling with. At the end of our exchange, Andrew accepted my offer to return the next day to see how he was. However, the following afternoon I found a new patient in what had previously been Andrew's bed. The ward sister then told me Andrew had slept through the night and was deemed well and relaxed enough to go home.

I have not described this spiritual care intervention merely because it had a positive outcome. It took place more than 16 years ago and still I return to it as a formative experience in my learning about human mortality, vulnerability, belief and finding meaning and hope in suffering.

Death is not always the worst that can happen in life. Indeed, as Andrew story shows, life itself can be felt to be worse than death, even with belief that there is no afterlife. Death can be a wished-for event even when, paradoxically, there are purposeful reasons to live – a relief in the face of enduring pain, lack of control or meaning, and feeling a constant burden. In addition, Andrew's story reinforces the significance of the contextual in doing pastoral theology. As I explored this encounter within a reflective practice group, I realized that resurrection was experienced (if not named) by Andrew – seemingly small glimpses of hope and new life in Andrew's particular circumstances were not just life enhancing but life changing. Resurrection in this context was Andrew being able to sleep peacefully even in a state of helplessness as he approached death, going home to be with someone he loved (even for a day) and finding hope for a short time before impending death even when there is no belief in an afterlife.

My time with Andrew, and with many other dying patients, has made me often fantasize and wonder about my own death and the death of those I love. For example, what death might be like and how I would cope with waiting for death if I were in a similar position to Andrew and Jeanie. My encounter with Andrew also challenged me to be honest about my beliefs and questions about the existence of an afterlife and what form I and others may take if there is a hereafter. This is an ongoing exercise which I return to informed by pastoral and personal experience in dialogue with the reading of Scripture and other theological disciplines as well as engagement with the arts, media and film. Far from being morbid, these are healthy and significant issues to consider for both deepening professional practice and living.[8]

In my teaching of divinity students, pastoral carers, nursing and medical students and practitioners, an exercise I often use to help us all intentionally consider our mortality and that of our significant others, is to read Roger McGough's poem *A Youngman's Death* aloud, and then to ask the participants to consider what for them would be a good death:

> Let me die a youngman's death
> not a clean and inbetween
> the sheets holywater death
> not a famous-last-words
> peaceful out of breath death

---

8 Of course, such fantasies become unhealthy if they dominate our thoughts and dreams and lead to suicidal ideation or intent, as part of depressive illness or in response to a sudden loss or bereavement. In such instances appropriate support should be sought.

When I'm 73
and in constant good tumour
may I be mown down at dawn
by a bright red sports car
on my way home
from an allnight party

Or when I'm 91
with silver hair
and sitting in a barber's chair
may rival gangsters
with hamfisted tommyguns burst in
and give me a short back and insides

Or when I'm 104
and banned from the Cavern
may my mistress
catching me in bed with her daughter
and fearing for her son
cut me up into little pieces
and throw away every piece but one

Let me die a youngman's death
not a free from sin tiptoe in
candle wax and waning death
not a curtains drawn by angels borne
'what a nice way to go' death. (2006, 42–3)

What amazes me is that people at different stages in life are, in the main, usually very willing to engage with the issue of their death and how it may happen. Indeed, invariably, we run out of time during a seminar or workshop in doing so. We discuss our reflections together and what quickly becomes obvious are the different ways people would like to die, based on their experience, engagement with the media and expressive arts as well as their familial, cultural and religious backgrounds. For some, a quick death with no long waiting to be endured would be preferable. Others would like some time in which to say goodbye and prepare their loved ones, knowing death was approaching. Most would want death to be painless, and for many it is important to die before they lose their faculties, control of bodily functions and become dependent on others. Some want to have a wake or party celebrating their life before they die and others would like to die with the minimum of fuss.

In order to facilitate a discussion about fears around death and dying, I then ask them what death they would not like and why. What often emerges are issues that Andrew struggled with as well as physical pain, unfinished or uncompleted tasks or business, a long lingering death with little quality of, or meaning and purpose in, life and being alone.

A deepening realization of our mortality through such exercises or our reflection on pastoral encounters with the ill, dying and bereaved may be a gift, albeit, paradoxically, an uncomfortable one to possess. A deepening realization that there truly is an end to our mortal existence as well as a beginning may in and of itself heighten meaning and purpose in our lives.

An awareness of our life being a gift of a limited timescale rather than a right to ongoing health and longevity may enable us to embrace life more fully in the present and all that each moment may offer us. Such an approach not only may heighten our attentiveness in relationships with others and open us to all that we may receive as well as offer; it will also enhance our relationships with the wonder of the natural world, the arts and ourselves. In all of these opportunities, in occurrences of mindfulness and times of full immersion in our human interactions and experience, we may glimpse something of God. Developing at least some acceptance of our mortality and vulnerability enables us not only to recognize our limitations but to enhance our ability to share grace-filled moments in caring relationships.

Scots poet and author Jackie Kay puts it another way as she reflects on her experience of hospitalization, alongside an elderly woman who is dying, after a moped accident in which she herself could have died. 'Getting close to death, it seems to whisper at the edge of your cheek. Nearly dying brings you closer to living. There's a thin border; you feel you cross it, going back to the land of the living, going home' (2010, 233).

Within the context of Psalm 90, which reminds us of our human frailties and limitations in comparison to the power and mystery of God, the writer asks God's help that we mortals may acknowledge the transitory nature of our earthly existence in order that we may grow in wisdom.[9] For the psalmist, owning our mortality can enhance our understanding, decision-making and way of living in the here and now. Our lives are framed by life and death. In the main, we cannot or choose not to determine the timing or nature of either, but we can influence what happens in between, how fulfilling our life may be and how it contributes to the lives of others and society in general. However, it remains our choice whether we seek to embrace, rather than keep at arm's length, our mortality. It is our decision to what extent we allow ourselves to be vulnerable with others, to be open to their stories (and all the joy and pain that may expose us to) as we journey with them through life towards their death, and ours. William Lawbaugh, an American professor of literature, reflecting on his experience of clinical pastoral education in an acute hospital concludes that it is important to:

prepare for death as much as possible and be prepared for death at all times. The fact that no one can be absolutely prepared and sustain that state of readiness for all of a lifetime should not deter us from trying our best. (2005, 25)

---

9   Psalm 90:12 – So teach us to count our days that we may gain a wise heart.

As for those whom we seek to love and care for, professionally and personally, they have to make their own judgements, including their attitude to the limitations of their life. In the end, we can only be responsible for ourselves, our way of being and relating and our approach to death and life.

9

Powerful Self

This chapter seeks to help readers to develop an awareness of the power and authority that they possess or have invested in them within caring relationships. Rowan Williams (2007), the current Archbishop of Canterbury, argues that Christians are disinclined to recognize the power we possess and, indeed, utilize within our daily lives. Much of Western culture, including the Church, tends to regard power more negatively than positively (Sims, 2008). Traditionally, pastoral theology has focussed more on the humility and compassion of Jesus rather than on his example of utilizing the power he possessed to enhance the well-being of others and challenge the oppressive religious and political structures and legislation of his day. There is a temptation to follow the Western ecclesial cultural norm of avoiding exploring issues of power in personal and professional relationships and in corporate political processes. To enable us to work as mature, effective and compassionate carers; however, we have to own and utilize, paradoxically, both the power and vulnerability we possess.

Whilst performing qualitative research with bereaved parents whose babies had died *in utero* by interviewing them about their experience of working with a chaplain, I was taken aback by the authority they invested in me as an academic researcher but also as a working chaplain. More than that, although the majority of these men and women had no affiliation with a local faith community, it was clear that they understood chaplains as possessing specialist knowledge, skills and experience, and thus, having authority and social status (Cameron et al., 2005, 40). This they respected and, at times, deferred to.[1] Irvine (1997) postulates that Western society is becoming increasingly indifferent to the role of clergy in wider society; however, within pastoral and spiritual care encounters as we seek to support vulnerable others, we, as church representatives, possess much power and influence. To what degree are we aware of this?

The issue is not whether pastoral and spiritual carers possess power. Rather it is about the choices we make in caring relationships to utilize our authority to best meet the perceived needs of the particular person or persons we are working with. It is not a bad thing to possess power; it is how we use it that is important.

Exploring a Typology of Power

There are, of course, different types of power in a variety of environments which may influence how a caring relationship is co-constructed or negotiated between a patient or parishioner and a practitioner. On one level, as in wider society, there is the kind of power we associate with military force, wealth, prestige and influence (based on Wells, 2007). On the other hand, power is also significant in one-to-one encounters with respect, for example, to the dynamics of sexuality, friendship and information sharing. The influence of power in different situations and matrices is complex and multi-faceted. For example, a pastoral relationship between a teenager living in an area of deprivation and an older minister may be influenced by the clergyperson's perceived relative wealth and intellect as well as by the manner in which he shows empathy and warmth in offering friendship (and his sensitivity to possible sexual undertones). American existential psychologist Rollo May describes a typology of power which together with

---

1   For a fuller account of these findings see Kelly (2007).

considering a relevant case study, may help further exploration of the influence of our power on the spiritual and
pastoral care we offer:

- *exploitative power* dominates, using force and coercion such
  as destructive criticism or threats;
- *manipulative power* controls in more subtle or disguised ways,
  such as exclusion from significant communication or using
  the other person to meet our need to be needed;
- *competitive power* is deeply ingrained in our culture, particularly in our political and economic systems. It can be positive
  and energizing when parties are relatively equal, for example
  in sport, but is destructive where there is an imbalance of
  power;
- *nutritive power* sustains and empowers, enabling the less powerful person to develop their own competence and freedom
  to act, as when adults enable children to do things for themselves, even if to start with they need help and support;
- *integrative power* respects the freedom of the other person and
  encourages their potential strengths; it involves relating to
  them as an equal, albeit with a different role, as in training
  relationship where the training incumbent brings skills and
  experience in ministry and the curate brings skills and experience from previous employment such as teaching. (1972,
  cited by Litchfield 2006, 39)

Jim was a probationary minister who had left divinity school
four months previously to start his new role as an assistant in
an urban parish, working with a more senior colleague. One
of his roles was to act as chaplain to one of the three local
primary schools in the parish. Very quickly, he established a
close bond with Tom, the new headmaster, who, though not a
'believer', was interested in helping the children in the school
understand the importance of the spiritual dimension in life
and in values-based learning. Besides that, both Jim and Tom
were keen cyclists and Jim sensed Tom liked to use him as a

sounding board, as they were both in their early thirties and finding their feet in their new roles.

Jim's senior colleague had been on summer holiday for over two weeks when he received a telephone call from the school secretary, who was a member of the church. Had Jim heard? Last night on cycling home from work, it appears Tom had collapsed, fallen off his bicycle and had been pronounced dead on arrival in hospital. Jim was horrified – what about Hazel, Tom's wife and his two children, Jack aged 12 and Holly aged 10? He had only briefly met Hazel once at a school function but he felt he should make contact.

Later in the afternoon, Jim, with great trepidation, pushed the family's doorbell. There was no reply but Jim left a note saying how sorry he was and his contact details. The next morning the phone rang – it was Hazel, thanking him for his thoughtfulness and asking him to come round as soon as he could. Jim rang the family's doorbell 20 minutes later, again filled with anxiety and fear – nothing at college had prepared him for this! Hazel answered the door and asked Jim in. As soon as he had sat down in the living room and before he could finish his condolences, Hazel began to bombard Jim with questions:

Why did Tom need to have a post-mortem?

How long would it take before the procurator fiscal could release Tom's body for the funeral?[2] When could Tom come home?

Which was the best undertaker to use locally? Who did Jim recommend?

Who could provide a coffin which was made of natural resources and was biodegradable?

Hazel had heard of woodland burial sites – where was the nearest one?

---

2   The equivalent of a coroner in Scotland.

Jack hadn't cried yet – was this normal and if not what effect would this have on him later?

Hazel herself felt she was numb, she couldn't take in what had happened and was fully aware she had gone into practical mode. She wanted to also know if this was normal.

By now, Jim's head was spinning and, as Hazel paused to draw breath, he suggested they might take these questions one at time. What about them having a cup of coffee as they did so?

As she sat down after giving Jim his coffee, Hazel began to cry. 'I've never done this before and I never expected to have to do it for Tom, not yet anyway. I feel totally lost and alone.' Jim gave her time to cry and eventually said, 'I'll help all I can and the undertaker will be a good help with the practical things. I don't know all the answers to your questions right now but I'll find out the information you need as soon as I can and get back to you. It'll help you make the decisions you want to for Tom, for yourself and your family. You see I'm not long in post as an assistant and my boss is on holiday. However, I got to know Tom and I really liked him. He was a good guy and a much-admired headmaster.'

'That's kind of you, I know Tom liked you. He mentioned you. But I thought you'd know all about funerals, making arrangements and bereavement. I mean I thought you'd know what's best.' Jim picked up her disappointment.

Hazel then began to talk about Tom and how they met, their courting and his love of cycling and the outdoors. After a while, Jack and Holly joined them. Jack remained silent for most of the time but Holly sat on her Mum's knee and joined in. Forty minutes later they made an arrangement for Jim to phone that evening with more information. Hazel and Jim would talk more then.

That afternoon, Jim phoned Angus, an older trusted friend who had been in ministry for many years in a nearby town. He was able to give Jim much of the information he required and some advice about supporting the bereaved. Jim also downloaded some material from the internet about bereavement, especially a couple of useful looking websites for children and teenagers.[3] However, before Jim could call Hazel back, the phone rang. It was Andrew, his senior colleague. He had returned home from his holiday a couple of days early and had heard about Tom tragic death. Jim talked a little about his involvement so far but before he could finish Andrew interrupted. Did Jim mind, but he, Andrew, thought it best if he stepped in and supported Hazel and the family now? It was such a traumatic situation, Jim was just out of college and it would be a big funeral. After all, Tom was a significant member of the community. Nothing against Jim or his pastoral inexperience, but this was a situation which needed sensitive handling.

Jim felt he could do little but agree under the circumstances. However, when he came off the telephone, he found himself not only bewildered but feeling sidelined and more than a bit angry. He had done his best in a difficult situation – what he needed was some support and encouragement, not to be belittled and undermined. Having talked it over with his wife, Jim later phoned his older friend and mentor Angus again to arrange to pop over and see him in a couple of days time.

After a church meeting the following evening, Jim asked Andrew how Hazel and her family were, and almost as an afterthought inquired how he had heard about Tom's sudden death. Andrew looked a bit sheepish. 'Oh, er, well terrible situation for Hazel . . . trying to reassure them that their feelings are all normal. As for hearing about Tom . . . well, I always ask the session clerk to call my mobile if anything major comes up. We are only in the caravan three hours away. Nothing to do

---

3 www.rd4u.org.uk – a website designed by bereaved teenagers for bereaved teenagers.
www.childbereavement.org.uk/for_young_people and www.winstonswish.org.uk have material for parents and young people.

with you – I do it every time I go away whether an assistant or a neighbouring minister is covering for me.'

Angus let Jim share his story and his feelings when they met over a coffee in Angus's study. The more experienced minister then sought to help the younger assistant explore some of the possible power issues involved in his relationship with Andrew. What Jim wanted was Andrew to use his power nutritively in their relationship. Jim would have welcomed Andrew's support, guidance and advice in supporting Hazel and her family, trusting and empowering him to work with the family to help him co-construct an appropriate funeral for Tom with them. Jim felt there was a real learning opportunity lost. Jim was angry about Andrew's manipulative use of power to keep him ignorant of communication between the session clerk and himself. He also realized that Andrew's inability to let go of pastoral control, even when on holiday, displayed his constant need to be needed. In addition, Angus also suggested that there may be some competitive power games being played by Andrew as he may see Jim, an able and warm young minister, as a threat.

However, Angus also helped Jim to reflect on his encounter with Hazel, Jake and Holly, and the power dynamics that may have been played out in that pastoral encounter. Jim realized that Hazel invested power and authority in him that he did not have. She expected Jim to have expert knowledge not only about the practical issues surrounding sudden death, but also regarding experience and knowledge of bereavement. If he had possessed such power, it would have been up to Jim as to how he used it to meet this particular family's needs (or, indeed, to primarily meet his needs). What was important, however, was that Jim did not pretend he had such authority and expertise – he was open and honest about this. The power dynamic then shifted in the relationship following Hazel's initial disappointment, and she and Holly then readily shared family stories about Tom. With further gentle encouragement by Angus, Jim also realized that he felt uncomfortable not having that power and that he tried to maintain control of the situation by stating he would go and find out the required information. In fact, he had in part behaved like Andrew by wanting to be needed, by seeking to regain his credibility and had not utilized his potential nutritive power. There had been an opportunity to empower the family to make their own enquiries about practical issues and bereavement information on the internet. Jim, in his eagerness to make himself useful, had not even asked if the family had wanted to do these things for themselves (though they may not have).

Utilizing Power – Responsibilities and Choices

Utilizing power in pastoral or spiritual care practice with the interest of the patient or practitioner at heart is not just simply the application of a set of moral rules or techniques. Nor is it merely responding to our instincts in the present moment. Elaine Graham, professor of Practical Theology at the University of Chester, says this of pastoral practice:

> It necessarily involves the inhabitation of communal conventions of speech, meaning and action. Even if one is acting in isolation, one's practice is governed by rules and systems of meaning which have been historically formed. Moral norms are thus built into practice; but equally, practice must be seen as an outworking and re-enactment of these values. The 'virtues' for MacIntyre (1987) are those values which enable us to give moral substance and direction to practice. That requires immersion in relationships of obligation and honesty with others; the practices that sustain and continue human culture are inconceivable without institutions or structures by which they are given tangible and external form. (2002, 99)

Graham, in referring to MacIntyre, is making two crucial points worth emphasizing in relation to ongoing appropriate use of power in pastoral practice.

First, that which significantly informs the care we offer others and the choices we make in doing so, is shaped by the influential communities in our formative years, where life-configuring narratives and practices have been experienced and absorbed. As Wells and Quash (2010, 193) simply yet profoundly state: 'Ethics becomes a matter less of making good decisions than of making good people. For it is good people that make good decisions'. As previously discussed in Chapter 5, for the pastoral or Christian spiritual carer, where we primarily learn how to use power responsibly (or not) is in the Church. It is the storied community where we hear, sing, share, eat and become part of the narrative which reveals how God empowers God's people. Duncan Forrester emphasizes the potential significance of worship on our practice and behaviour:

> Worship should shape and enrich practice and the ethics of the community of faith . . . Christian worship . . . is the heart of Christian practice and ethics, which expresses the significance of the whole and sustains and illumines the Christian life. In worship and in action which flows from it we learn how to be Christians; and in doing we explore the nature and claim of faith. (1997, 46)

In the worship and life of our home faith community, we absorb habits about how to use power, which we in turn act out and utilize for good or ill in our personal and professional relationships. Clergy, especially those who regularly lead or facilitate worship, have their status and authority within faith communities re-affirmed on a weekly basis as informed interpreters of Scripture and ordained administers of the sacraments. Without regular accountability within supervision, such power can become a potential threat to the empowerment and enablement of others' liberation and well-being in worship, in other leadership or mentoring contexts and pastoral encounters (LaMothe, 2005).

This is the second important point Graham is making in relation to the moral dimension of pastoral practice. The manner in which Andrew misuses power in his capacity as Jim's senior colleague is habitual and he will continue to act in such manipulative and competitive ways unless he takes the opportunity to regularly and intentionally reflect on his practice with an honest and insightful other. Such critical conversations can help our decision-making habits to be re-visited and refined, to become more virtuous. By doing so, we too, can contribute to community or institutional cultures (e.g., ecclesial or healthcare), which in turn shape corporate and individual character, behaviours and practices for the good.

The concept of *phronesis* was introduced in Chapter 3 as an accumulated practical wisdom which, when employed with discernment, can enhance the betterment of another's wellbeing in the context of caring relations. *Phronesis* develops through ongoing reflective practice. It enables good choices to be made and power to be utilized benevolently, when a practitioner combines both moral reasoning and the desire to care (Pembroke, 2007). Such practical wisdom is key to understanding how we use power, at times, to control others and situations as a distraction from aspects of ourselves which are uncomfortable and threatening. In utilizing influence and authority over others, we may avoid having to look within ourselves and deal with things which we feel powerless or uncomfortable about. In his poem *The Little Ways That Encourage Good Fortune*, William Stafford helps develop this theme:

> Wisdom is having things right in your life
> and knowing why.
> if you do not have things right in your life
> you will be overwhelmed:
> you may be heroic, but you will not be wise.
> If you have things right in your life
> but do not know why,

you are just lucky, and you will not move
in the little ways that encourage good fortune.

The saddest are those not right in their lives
who are acting to make things right for others:
they act only from the self –
and that self will never be right:
no luck, no help, no wisdom. (1977, 234)

None of us will ever have our lives completely sorted or right
yet unless we are aware that our decision-making and use
of power may be something we hide our true selves behind,
then Stafford is right; our situation is sad – for ourselves and
for those we seek to care for.

Phronesis is one of several virtues which when embodied,
enacted and utilized sensitively in caring relationships will help
us to habitually make good decisions. Others include integrity,
courage, patience, empathy, humility, faith (not necessarily
a religious faith but, for example, faith in others or oneself),
hope and temperance (Robinson, 2008). For Leeds-based ethicist Simon Robinson, these traits of our moral character are
habituated (as well as having a gifted or given dimension) not
just from our experience of institutions and faith communities,
but rather from significant formative and ongoing relationships. Importantly, we can also develop morally by reflecting
on what we learn from those we seek to support in caring relationships. For example, Hazel's ability to enable or empower
Holly to share her stories of her deceased dad and to allow Jack
to be as he needed to be during their encounter with Jim, were
lessons about the use of power which Jim could learn from and
replicate to his and others' benefit.

Part III

Sustaining Self

10

Meaningful Self

There is nothing that pastors do for the congregation that is more important than taking care of their own souls. (Barnes 2009, 56)

If we are to help others find meaning and purpose in life, can we do so without having an awareness of what nurtures, invigorates and brings us to life? If we are to enable healing and restoration in others, how aware are we of what soothes our soul and aids us in our journey towards wholeness? How much time and space do we intentionally make to meet our own spiritual needs? For if this not a priority, as Barnes suggests, what inner resources will we have to care for others in our professional and private lives, let alone ourselves?

What gives us direction and fulfilment in life will not be the same for us as for the next person, but to reflect on such things is not only a reminder that we need to invest in, and attend to, meaningful activities. In addition, it gives us an appreciation of how significant the spiritual dimension is for enabling human resilience and flourishing.

When assessing the spiritual needs of a patient in a healthcare setting, I ask such questions as:

- What in life is important to you right now?
- What raises your spirits?
- What gets you up in the morning and keeps you going through the day?
- What makes you feel alive?
- When the chips have been down in the past, what has helped you?

These are tools which we might utilize periodically for ourselves in order to help us attend to the significant elements of our lives which enable us not just to survive as spiritual and pastoral carers but to positively thrive.

We need to find what gives our particular lives meaning and purpose and not just rely on 'received' meaning from authority figures in our formative years. To live a life merely enabling vicarious fulfilment or to prioritize meeting the needs of others in our personal or family lives is to suppress the expression of our true selves. Daryl Paulson, in an article entitled *The Search for Spiritual Authenticity*, gets to the heart of the matter:

> To discover ultimate meaning for oneself requires self-inquiry, self-awareness, courage, faith and risk (Bugental, 1981). When escape and avoidance overrule authentic choice, one has essentially committed psychospiritual suicide (Antony et al., 1987). This situation is described vibrantly in Fyodor Dostoevsky's (1949, 191) novel *The Brothers Karamozov*. In the novel, Christ returns to the people, bringing them the freedom and love they have sought for so long. But Christ is arrested by the Church's Grand Inquisitor and is to be burnt at the stake the following day as the worst of heretics. The night before His death, the Grand Inquisitor visits Christ in His dungeon cell. Greatly perplexed, he asks Christ why He came back to the people, because they do not want what He gives. The Inquisitor says to Christ:

> "Thou wouldst go into the world, and art going with empty hands, with some promise of freedom which men in their simplicity and their native unruliness cannot even understand, which they fear and dread – for nothing has ever been more insupportable for men and human society than freedom."

> The Inquisitor explains that what the masses want the Church provides – security – not what Christ

provides – love and freedom. The masses he says, want to be told what makes them safe. (2006, 198–9)

The search to find authentic meaning and purpose in our lives is to discover for ourselves what liberates us to really be ourselves. As St Irenaeus stated, 'The glory of God is the human person most fully alive' (cited in Au and Cannon 1995, 2). Such living and praising of God is not found in feeling or playing safe, nor having the aim in life to make others feel likewise.

Finding Meaning in Doing

Vocational Caring

To find meaning and purpose in providing spiritual and pastoral care is to fulfil a vocational role. It is indeed a special thing, a gift to be treasured and nurtured; not everybody performs significant roles in their lives – especially ones which dominate their waking hours during the week – which they find fulfilling. To find meaning in any role is to be able to utilize our particular God-given gifts to the best of our ability in the context in which we are working. Caring for another is never completely altruistic; part of our motivation is undoubtedly to fulfil our need to be needed and a means to find purpose and fulfilment. W.H. Auden, in his poem *As I Walked Out One Evening*, puts it this way:

You shall love your crooked neighbour with your crooked heart. (cited by Heaney and Hughes 1981, 41)

Those who choose to enter into a professional caring role do not merely do so for purely benevolent reasons, nor solely for the salary or stipend. There is a need within all of us who work with the sick, dying or distressed not only to improve the quality of living or (dying) of others, but also to make us feel better about ourselves. As Campbell states, 'Unless we recognize the element of personal need leading people into professional caring, we shall fail to see how damaging some forms of over-commitment can be' (for both carer and cared for) (1984, 105). The need within a carer to constantly attempt to rescue others from their perceived plight not only disempowers the cared for but indicates a carer with a low sense of worth and well being; a person who needs to prove her worth (to herself and those around her) by making things better for others. The really needy individual in such a case is the helper, not the helped, who, if they recognize their neediness, may well require the support of a trusted and skilled other to explore the source(s) of their low self-esteem and loneliness. For example, Terry, the chaplain in Chapter 6 who sought solace in work as a way to avoid facing the pain of his marital breakdown.

Parishioners and patients may feel indebted to a pastoral or spiritual carer for their support:

> But the professional, who is aware of how much he or she gains in support, enlightenment and personal development from helping others, may well feel a greater indebtedness. It is often more blessed to care than to be cared for; and the ability to care is frequently made possible by the understanding and sensitivity of the needy person. (Campbell, 1984, 106)

However, if our identities are solely defined by our vocational role, then we have lost touch with who we really are. Being fully alive and fulfilled involves far more in life than embodying a caring role.

Play

Margaret Kornfield, an American pastoral psychotherapist, emphatically extols the virtues of creativity and play to enable pastoral and spiritual carers to thrive in their vocational and personal lives. She says those who do so:

> give in to delight. Think of those counselors whom you know who also *find life interesting*. They have a passion for their *avocations*. They are true *amateurs*, who love and develop their interest in art, photography, music, piloting a plane, or climbing a mountain. They are involved in some way with the world, with creation, with creating. They do not need to live through others for excitement. They live with thanksgiving. (1998, 303)

Seamus Heaney echoes such creativity in the form of writing or engaging with poetry. He describes it as a means of compensating for events in the rest of life or restoring equilibrium in response to difficulties or challenges. 'This redressing effect of poetry comes from its being a glimpsed alternative, a revelation of potential that is denied or constantly threatened by circumstances' (Heaney cited by Astley, 2002, 22). To have playful or creative opportunities in our lives is to have the taste of something more, something different, enlivening and nurturing, which is vital for our well-being. It is the very stuff that makes life worth living. Expressing our creativity and playfulness can take many forms – from painting, singing and dancing, to taking part in sport, gardening or writing poetry. However we play and (re)discover delight in life, we need to take time to do so and cherish and protect such time. Michael Hare-Duke, a bishop within the Scottish Episcopal Church, in the poem *Playtime*, revealed his understanding of the intentional necessity of such counter-cultural activity:

> It takes a kind of courage
> to find time for play.
> Work is what's expected; sober thoughts,
> a misership of time hoarding the precious minutes.

Fun yields no dividends,
no bonuses for jokes.
Work earns the wages;
the jobless are devalued.

Computer-haunted,
we've got it wrong.
Machines are made to whir and turn
faultless, precise, achieving;
the human spirit should have space to soar
to wild absurdity.
We need permission to uncage our poet.
Eyes that rest on beauty
seem ineffectual compared to hands that
hammer.
Yet I take time off
from industrious striving
to watch, enjoy my friendships, delight in
touch and taste
nourish my true self.

Dreams, imagination and God's laughter in
creation,
invite me out of my industrious solemnity,
to take the task of playing seriously
until my marred manhood
is recreated in the child I have denied. (1994, 76–7)

Relationships

In asking patients or their relatives what is sustaining for them
in times of ill health or anxiety, they often talk about their partners, families and close friends, people who love them, care for
them and accept them as they are, no matter what. Such relationships are priceless and the source of great strength, support
and meaning in our lives. However, for many who are busy
caring for others, sometimes these relationships get second
best in terms of our time, attention and energy. Ray Anderson

helpfully emphasizes the significance of such sustaining and nurturing relationships to our well-being:

> As caregivers, many of us lack the kind of nourishing love which we seek to give to others. It is one thing to meditate on the Scriptures which remind us of the love God has for us. We need more than that. We need and must cultivate relationships in which we are the recipients of the kind of love which we provide others. It is not a sign of weakness to need the love of others to be expressed in tangible, personal ways . . . the words of John MacMurray (1961, 150) are relevant here as a source of nourishment for the inner self: 'I need you to be myself. This need is for a fully positive personal relation in which, because we trust one another, we can think and feel and act together. Only in such a relation can we really be ourselves.' (2004, 107)

The intimacy of such relationships requires time to be established, as well as trust and mutuality to be developed (Jacques, 2004, 21). There is a solidity and sense of security to them which provides a feeling of rootedness and belonging, as well as an affirmation and lightness of touch which engenders risk taking and reflection. Such relationships are the foundations which enable us to stretch and grow – the home to which we can return, to receive warmth and nurture.

Worship

In Chapter 5 we explored how the Church is the primary community where our identities as pastoral and spiritual carers from the Christian tradition are formed and shaped in relationship. Worship as an integral activity in our weekly rhythm helps practitioners to continue to hone and reform who we are and how we relate. It affords us the opportunity to communally express and renew our faith as well as to question and grow. In worship, we have the opportunity to deepen our self-understanding of who we are as God's people, both corporately and individually.

Writing in a Scottish context, Forrester et al. describe the activity of worship as:

> the offering of the whole of life; our relationship to God cannot be confined in one compartment of our lives. Times of service are important if we are to offer the service of our lives; the special times to sustain and deepen the constant relationship . . . In worship God is encountered and glorified. God's purposes are discerned, however faintly, and God's people are nourished and strengthened for service. (1996, 3)

American and English Christian ethicists Stanley Hauwerwas and Sam Wells, emphasize the significance of the centrality of worship not only in the moral development of God's people, but how through regular participation in worship we might find meaning in our living and relating:

> Worship is the time when God trains his people to imitate him in habit, instinct and reflex . . . worship trains God's people to be examples of what his love can do . . . Over and over, God's people see the way God's Son took, blessed, broke, and gave, so that this pattern might give life to the world. (2004, 25)

Finding Meaning in Being

I am not there
I am not then
I am nowhere else
but here.
I am not them

I am not you
I am myself.

I rest from doing,
need not achieve.
I do not ask
I do not need.
This is the place
for me to be.

Here I am (*Dwelling*, Rudd, 2010, 3)

Contemplative Self

it has taken half a lifetime
to learn to sit in the sun
among primroses and violets
beside a dried adder skin
your back to a broken wall (from *The Hundred
Thousand Places,* Clark, 2009, 84)

The ability, or not, to be still and silent may be a gauge as to
what extent we are comfortable with being who we are, with
living in our own skin, and the degree of disquiet or stress
in our lives at any one time. In being still and being quiet on
our own, we not only have the opportunity to observe the
primroses and violets around us and enjoy the warmth of the
sun, we are also faced with ourselves. In silence, Mosse (2003)
argues we may experience restlessness, anxiety and a real need
to move onto the next task, project or activity. Experiencing
such 'loneliness' (Mosse, 2003, 80, based on Merton, 1972)
indicates a dis-ease with self at a particular time or stage in life's
journey. On the other hand, in quiet and stillness we may feel a
sense of connectedness or well being and a desire to hold onto
and carry such moments of 'solitude' within us as resources to
utilize when life becomes stressful and self is disjointed and
lonely. As Mosse helpfully describes 'these two experiences of

being alone are not static states; they form a spectrum along which we can move. . .' (2003, 80). Practising spending time alone, being attentive to the world around us and within does not come easily to most of us who are caught up the contemporary world of productivity and achieving, as Clark's poem suggests. However, making regular, intentional time and space to be still and silent not only creates a context in which we may grow in self-awareness, it can help us note the patterns of our inner response to exposure to self. In seeking silence and time apart alone, we do not escape from the world, but the very opposite; we are forced to square up to our world of thoughts, feelings and reflections on our actions. As humans, we will never on our earthly journey always or completely feel at ease with ourselves. However, if 'solitude' is what we tend to experience rather than anxiety when quiet and alone, then we are fortunate indeed, and if not, perhaps the need for quiet and stillness requires increased priority in the rhythm of our life, as well as the support of a trusted other.

Jean Vanier, the French-Canadian spiritual writes of the renewing power of silence for him:

> My three weeks stay in the monastery is coming to an end. I was tired when I arrived, as the month of July had been quite heavy. I immediately entered into silence, which is a milieu or atmosphere that gives me new life. I felt like a fish in water and I really drank of the water of silence. I rediscovered time, not as a space too small for everything that has to be fitted in, but time as a touch of eternity, a presence which, like silence, is a milieu, a place for communion and intimacy that always goes beyond time. Now I feel rested and blessed . . . I feel ready to go back into daily life, back into the world of struggle and pain, the world of injustice and evil. That does not mean that here in the monastery I have not been in touch with all that is dark and painful within my own heart. (2008, 156)

Not all of us are like Vanier and easily transfer from the hustle and bustle of our working life into solitude and silence. Many of us find such a counter-cultural intention – being quiet and still in our own company – a huge challenge. We may be extraverted by nature or may never have got into the habit of periods of non-goal-orientated activity. If we are honest, we may be frightened by what might surface if our veneer of busyness and achieving is cast aside for a while (what Vanier calls dark and painful). Such fantasies and happenings are indeed anxiety-inducing and hard to face, yet are opportunities for our shadow to be explored, even embraced, in the company of a loving, trusted other.

Andrew Greig, in his poem *Down by the Riverside*, reminds us that meaningfulness in silence can be captured in moments of time not just in days of solitude. In attending to such moments we may glimpse something more:

> Standing under trees in light
> rain, end of winter, more than
> half way through my life.
>
> Thought, movement,
> the pauses in between . . .
>
> The swollen river lips
> the bank, the branches bead
> and something stops.
> It comes clear: time
> doesn't flow, it drips.
>
> And here's eternities between the drops.
> (2006b, 167)

Such eternities are not encountered and enjoyed unless we are open and prepared to encounter them. As the prophet Isaiah informs the Israelites, the ground needs to be made ready before something of the transcendent, beyond time, is experienced.[1] In the ebb and flow of our lives, there requires to be a regular rhythm of activity, interspersed with stillness; of being a part of and apart from, to make room for eternity to be glimpsed and enjoyed in the constant flux of the here and now. Otherwise, life will seem to flow away from us and its meaning and purpose will remain elusive. It is in these moments of transcendence which take us beyond loss and pain, striving and strife, that enable us to face the challenges of the present and the uncertainty of the future.

Attention to the Moment

Those who have the gift of attention to the other and to our inner selves in the moment make the best poets as well as pastors. However, there is a need to hone, nurture and enjoy such abilities (see also Chapter 3). For poet Kathleen Jamie, this is done by weaving her attentiveness to the natural world into her daily routine. In her perceptive book *Markings*, she describes observing the birds in her neighbourhood.

> Myself, I keep the binoculars about me, and catch a glance at coffee-time, or before fetching the children to school . . . Between the laundry and the fetching kids from school, that's how birds enter my life. I listen. During a lull in the traffic, oyster catchers. In the school playground, sparrows – what few sparrows there are left – chirp from the eaves. (2005, 38–9)

Weaving such moments of intentional attentiveness to life, external and internal, into our day not only develops our

---

1 'A voice cries out: "In the wilderness prepare the way of the Lord, make straight in the desert, a highway for our God. Every valley shall be lifted up, and every mountain and hill be made low; the uneven ground shall become level and the rough places a plain. Then the glory of the Lord shall be revealed, and all the people shall see it together, for the mouth of the Lord has spoken."' Isaiah 40: 3–5.

natural abilities but also affords opportunities for grace-filled, life-enhancing moments.

Attentiveness is also at the heart of prayer and our relationship with God, seeking to discern God's presence or voice around us or within us. Ann Lewin's poem *Disclosure* captures this beautifully:

> Prayer is like watching for the
> Kingfisher. All you can do is
> Be where he is likely to appear, and
> Wait.
> Often,
> Nothing much happens;
> There is space, silence and expectancy.
> No visible sign, only the
> Knowledge that he's been there
> And may come again.
> Seeing or not seeing cease to matter.
> You have been prepared.
> But when you've almost stopped
> Expecting it, a flash of brightness
> Gives encouragement. (2009, 31)

Rest

It is often in our down time, when we let our minds and imaginations wander, that often the most unexpected yet potentially profound insights or daydreams drift into our consciousness. Our most creative and potentially transformative moments are gifted to us when our psyches are not straining and our days are uncluttered with activity and striving. This poem by Sonja Rose, called the *Eighth Day*, strikes a chord:

> I declare today
> The eighth day of the week,
> Freed of oughts and shoulds and even musts,
> A holiday, a holy day,

A gift without strings,
A time-space to savour,
To expand into rooms long neglected
And linger there,
Patiently,
Watching for unknown buds to flower –

Welcome them,
Though they may startle
With dark,
Unexpected blooms. (2008, 4)

There is a story told of St Anthony, one of the renowned desert fathers of the third and fourth centuries, which encapsulates the need for balance or a sustainable rhythm in the life of those who enable others to search for inner resources and wisdom:

> Once the great Anthony of the Desert was relaxing with his disciples outside his hut when a hunter came by. The hunter was surprised to see Anthony relaxing, and rebuffed him for taking it easy. It was not his idea of what a holy monk should be doing.
>
> Anthony replied, 'Bend your bow and shoot an arrow.'
>
> And the hunter did so.
>
> 'Bend it again and shoot another arrow,' said Anthony.
>
> The hunter did so, again and again.
>
> The hunter finally said, 'Abba Anthony, if I keep my bow always stretched it will break.'
>
> 'So it is with the monk,' replied Antony. 'If we push ourselves beyond measure, we will break. It is right from time to time to relax our efforts.'[2]

---

2 Taken from Au and Cannon (1995, 111)

Building in relaxation and play, retreat and sabbatical into the pattern of our lives and pages of our diaries is crucial to revive our spirits, rest our bodies and prevent our bow from breaking. This means planning ahead and making our restorative and spiritual needs a priority. It means truly believing we are beloved and that nurturing and loving ourselves as our neighbours is not ego-centric or a sin, but is to follow Christ.

Jesus was by nature and necessity both social and solitary, enabling meaning and purpose to be found in his life and ministry in being with and being alone. After feeding the five thousand, Jesus made his disciples go on ahead of him and he dismissed the crowd. 'After saying farewell to them, he went up on to the mountain to pray.'[3]

In order for our caring to continue to be fulfilling for ourselves and significant for those we care for, and our lives to have depth and meaning, we need to develop as practitioners and human beings in an ongoing and creative manner over time.

Developing Self

If you live long enough, you realise you are not the person you were.

(Graber, 2010, cited by Kellaway, 2010, 43).

How do we develop our self-understanding in an ongoing manner that enhances our practice and well-being? This is a key question for all spiritual and pastoral carers if we are to deliver not only proficient and compassionate care but maintain our motivation and ability to care over the long haul. At the core of any sufficient response to this question is reflective practice. It is not in simply relating to others that we become who we are. It is rather through reflection on practice which

---

3   Mark 6: 46

takes seriously the context and culture in which we are working, as well as the content and the form of our encounters that
we may deepen our understanding of who we are becoming.

This final section is not intended to be a thorough exploration of reflective practice – others do this far more rigor-
ously elsewhere.[4] Its function, rather, is to emphasize that
such activity in various forms, is essential for practitioners to
be persons who can continue to offer an informed therapeutic
presence to others in times of difficulty and distress over a
significant period. Without regular, rigorous reflective practice, the quality of the attention and care we offer others will
stagnate and suffer.

Developing Self-Awareness

A crucial element in enabling an ongoing, deepening understanding of self and how we relate to others and to God, is the
establishment of relationships with trusted others which have
an explicit understanding that these issues are the *raison d'etre*
for the relationship itself. The people whose company we seek
out, and may indeed enter formal covenants or contracts with,
to enable us to intentionally reflect on our practice with them
are not just friends or acquaintances. They are people who
have natural abilities, training, experience, skills and knowledge that enable them to create a safe space in which we can
explore our practice and its impact on our personhood: our
beliefs, values and self-understanding. R. S. Thomas's poem
Groping points to the heart of this:

> Moving away is only to the boundaries
> of the self. Better to stay here,
> I said, leaving the horizon
> clear. The best journey to make
> is inward. It is the interior

---

4   Readers may want to follow up references in this chapter to engage more
deeply with various approaches to reflective practice.

that calls. Eliot heard it.
Wordsworth turned from the great hills
of the north to the precipice
of his own mind, and let himself
down for the poetry stranded
on the bare ledges.
                          For some
it is all darkness; but for me, too,
it is dark. But there are hands
there I can take, voices to hear
solider than the echoes
without. And sometimes a strange light
shines, purer than the moon,
casting no shadow, that is
the halo upon the bones
of the pioneers who died for truth. (1993,
328)

Whose are the possible hands that can take ours to help us journey into the darkness of our interior and the solid voices to listen to?[5]

Holy Friendships

The concept of 'holy friendships' (Jones and Armstrong, 2006), is more than just having a buddy with whom we can trust ourselves and our faith and doubts. These are companions who not only share life and glimpses of the transcendent along the road, but also have the desire to understand our unique perceptions and perspectives. In addition, such friends are willing, with integrity, to help deepen our engagement with self, God and experience. Such friendships involve reciprocity, a desire for truth-telling (even when it is tough for both to do so), mutual

---

5   The various roles described here of people who may help us in our journey of self-discovery are not discrete. Some or much of their function may be performed by a supportive other who carries a different label.

respect and love. A colleague, Michael Paterson, in fact, uses the term 'critical lovers' to describe such relationships. Holy friends, critical lovers or critical conversation partners are in it for the long haul. They want fulfilment and meaning for each other not just in the relationship but also in both of their lives. Mentorship may be another term to refer to some such relationships, though it is usually applied to ones where a more experienced or mature reflective practitioner has a developing partnership with a more junior colleague. Edward Sellner cites Daniel Levison, a Yale psychology professor, in describing the most important function of a mentor as '*a facilitator of the other person's dream*, the vision of self and the life he or she wants to lead as an adult' (1990, 25). While such an arrangement contains mutuality and opportunities for growth and learning by both parties, the power in such a relationship is undoubtedly asymmetrical. Such relationships may be mandatory for trainee or newly appointed pastors. However, they are inevitably most creative and fulfilling for both, if each has a say in whom they work with – both junior practitioner and mentor.

Spiritual Directors

A spiritual director or 'soul friend' may particularly help us to explore our relationship with God in our daily lives, including our spiritual and pastoral care practice. In such a relationship, the focus is on discerning God's presence and intention. Thus, discernment and openness to where God may be and what God intends for us in terms of vocation or direction in life, is at the centre of such a relationship. Jean Stairs, a Canadian pastoral theologian says this of spiritual direction:

In my experience, people can name the ways God is present if they are invited to do so. Without the purposeful invitation, however, the ways of the Spirit are generally not self-evident. Often they are subtle, unobtrusive, hidden in the midst of daily events and interactions. It takes practice to see and identify the grace of God in everyday life. So, listening for the soul means paying attention to the signs of God's voice and graceful activity and inviting others to become more aware of God speaking through such signs. (2000, 29)

Pastoral Supervisors

Pastoral supervision involves the exploration of the interface between a practitioner's personal and vocational identities. It may include elements of spiritual direction and pastoral care but the locus of attention is the self at work.[6] It focuses on our understanding of our caring role, our desire or calling to perform that role and how we enact our particular vision in a specific context (Leach and Paterson, 2010). Such attention and engagement can be facilitated by a supervisor in a one-to-one relationship or in group settings. Whilst mentorship may help new practitioners to develop a vision of self in a caring role, pastoral supervision attends to that vision over time (Paterson and Leach, 2010) – exploring, refining and potentially deepening it. Kenneth Pohly writes of pastoral supervision within an American context:

Pastoral supervision is a method of doing and reflecting on ministry in which a supervisor (teacher) and one or more supervisees (learners) covenant together to reflect critically on their ministry as a way of growing in self-awareness, ministering competence, theological understanding, and Christian commitment. (1993, 75)

Supervision enables a practitioner to safely, creatively and purposefully utilize self as a therapeutic resource within caring relationships. Supervision as a mandatory, not just normative,

---

6 Should a supervisee's personal emotional or spiritual issues dominate the supervisory relationship over a period, then referral of the supervisee to a pastoral counsellor or spiritual director may be appropriate.

requirement for pastoral and spiritual care practitioners is both morally necessary and theologically informed. Believing we are beloved by God, just as those we support are, means taking seriously our well-being as much as theirs, and the development of ourselves, and our self-understanding, as people and practitioners.

Reflective Writing

I do not know what I know until I have said it, or written it down. (cited by Carroll, 2009)

Learning by reflection on practice is not just done through the spoken word. Reflective writing in different forms also affords practitioners the opportunity to deepen our self-awareness.

The journal of Logan Mountstuart forms the core of William Boyd's novel *Any Human Heart*. In his musings, Mountstuart lays out not only his reflections on his professional life as a writer, spy and art-dealer but explores his experience of what it is to be a human who is constantly developing and understanding more about the variety of roles he embodies and enacts. Such deepening of awareness through keeping a record of lived experience and the thoughts, feelings, fantasies and dreams they invoke, as Boyd describes, is done in a far from linear and organized fashion:

> We keep a journal to entrap that collection of selves that form us. Think of our progress through time as one of those handy images that illustrate the Ascent of Man. You know the type: diagrams that begin with the shaggy ape and his ground-grazing knuckles, moving on through slowly straightening and depilating hominids, until we reach the clean shaven Caucasian nudist proudly clutching the haft of his stone axe or spear. All the intervening orders assume a form of inevitable progression towards

this brawny ideal. But our human lives aren't like that, and true journal presents us with a more riotous and disorganised reality. The various stages of development are there, but they are jumbled up, counterposed and repeated randomly. The selves jostle for prominence in these pages: the mono-browed Neanderthal shoulders aside axe-wielding *Homo sapiens*; the neurasthenic intellectual trips up the bedaubed aborigine. It doesn't make sense; the logical perceived progression never takes place. The true *journal intime* understands this fact and doesn't try to posit any order or hierarchy, doesn't try to judge or analyse: I am all these different people – all these different people are me. (2003, 7)

In any one encounter with another, I can be carer and cared for, behave as a mature, responsible adult and be put in touch with the little child within. I may enter a relationship intending to utilize the authority invested in me by Church, a caring institution, university or by a parishioner and as that relationship evolves, become a learner, fellow sojourner and seeker. Yet at other times may enact the role of discerning guide or wise teacher depending on my need, how I perceive the need of the other and what the other invests in me. A journal may be a tool which enhances our awareness and deepens our understanding of the roles we perceive we have, the roles we co-construct with others for ourselves and them, and the roles they demand or require of us.

Journaling may enable more introverted individuals to express and layout aspects of their inner selves which they would not easily articulate to another, even in confidence. The writer Susan Sontag conveys the potential significance of journaling for not just the deepening of an understanding of identity but for formation of self:

Superficial to understand the journal as just a receptacle for one's private, secret thoughts – like a confidante who is deaf, dumb and illiterate. In the journal I do not just *express* more openly than I could to any person; I *create* myself.

The journal is a vehicle for my sense of selfhood. It represents me as emotionally and spiritually independent. Therefore (alas), it does not simply record my actual, daily life but rather – in many cases – offers an alternative to it. (2006, 7)

Journaling can also be a helpful way of noticing and naming losses before they become accumulative and harmful. It can be a helpful way of monitoring patterns of our mood, our energy levels and ability to engage in meaningful ways with others. If we, or those with whom we share our journal writings and inner selves, observe warning signs of disengagement or weariness, we can then take restorative action. Different practitioners find alternative creative ways to process and name loss before it becomes a burdensome load, for example through writing poetry or enactment in ritual (see Chapter 7).

Gillian Bolton, writing from within a healthcare context, enthuses about the writing of our stories as they unfold and the stories of our encounters with others as reflective resources which aid our ongoing development and self-awareness:

Reflective practice writing is a way of expressing and exploring our own and others' stories: crafting and shaping to aid understanding and development. These stories are data banks of skill, knowledge and experience: much of our knowing is in our doing. We can learn from our own and each other's mistakes and successes, each other's ideas, experience and wisdom, and tackle and come to terms with our own problem areas. Although practice is continually aired – over a coffee with a colleague – we do not tell each other or ourselves the things at the cutting edge of our difficulty. (2005, 23)

Such blind spots can be identified and explored by the sharing of our reflective writings and discussing them with others on a one-to-one basis, such as with a mentor or pastoral supervisor or in reflective practice groups. For example, the use of verbatim records of pastoral encounters can be role played in reflective practice groups and utilized as a focus for group reflection and learning.[7] Significant questions to ask ourselves when reflecting on a verbatim or another form of reflective writing are:

- What does this encounter or situation tell me about me?
- What does it tell me about my pastoral ability?
- How does it challenge or affirm my faith, beliefs and values?
- Whose need(s) is being met in this encounter or situation?

Theological Reflection on Practice

Theological reflection on practice is to let our experience creatively engage with our personal beliefs and values, and it is an activity which enables our historical tradition and our contextual understanding of that rich resource to inform that dialogue. It can be part of all the relationships and reflective activities outlined in this section. Engaging in theological reflection on practice does not necessarily mean a greater understanding of God's work in the world either through us, through others or human experience. Nor does it mean we immediately become more theologically mature or sophisticated. In other words; there is no 'quick fix. There are no guarantees. There is only the faithful longing and wrestling

---

7   For fuller accounts of the use of verbatums as part of reflective practice, see: (Not in References) Foskett and Lyall (1990), Ward (2005) and Leach and Paterson (2010).

that can discern from time to time, God's gracious presence which is often hidden and obscure' (Ballard, 2008, 288). For theological reflection on practice to truly enrich our journey of faith and impact with meaning on our future care of others it, therefore, has to be performed on an ongoing basis. It has to become an integral part of the rhythm of our working lives, not merely an occasional add-on or extra. Such intentional engagement with Scripture, tradition and doctrine as part of our ongoing pilgrimage is *habitus* – the gradual absorption of practical wisdom and growth in discernment, through a commitment to take regular time apart to reflect with others on who we are, how we act and what we share with others, whilst utilizing the resources of our faith.

The challenge not to see practical theological reflection as isolated or separate from other modes of theological learning. It is often when working across the boundaries of theological disciplines, which are often so specifically demarcated as very separate entities in academic circles, that our most creative and meaningful insights are made. For example, the methodology and writing of feminist and liberation theologians has much to offer reflective practitioners seeking to develop their awareness of self, social context and God. All that being said, David Lyall, a Scottish pastoral theologian, reminds us that theological reflection is not merely an intellectual exercise but is more a matter of 'personal integration' (2001, 37). Theological reflection on practice is not about doing applied theology – reading or absorbing the theology of others, no matter how erudite, inclusive or convincing. It is about forming and reforming our own beliefs and values based on our experience of offering spiritual or pastoral care. Lyall goes on to say:

> Our working theologies are highly personal constructs. We normally find ourselves within denominational families where we may identify ourselves with general theological positions and are happy to confess our

general allegiance to their traditions and statements of faith. Nevertheless, the actual working theologies which drive our actions are shaped not by creedal statements (certainly not by creedal statements alone) but by our experience of life. Within each of us there is a continuous internal dialogue taking place as we seek to relate present beliefs to fresh experience, allowing the emergence of a developing personal theology. (2001, 37)

In Christian circles, as in wider society, there can be the perception that time spent on reflection on self and self-in-relationship can be somewhat self-indulgent, narcissistic even, and is a way of avoiding the real world and work of ministry. On the contrary, not only are the relationships which are played out in the world to be found within the dynamics of the interior of self[8] but, attention to the development of knowledge of self is also to seek betterment for those we strive to care for. As Carl Jung described:

One *must* occupy oneself with oneself; otherwise one does not grow, otherwise one can never develop. One must plant a garden and give it increasing attention and care if one wants vegetables; otherwise only weeds flourish . . . Meditation on one's own being is an absolutely legitimate, even necessary activity if one strives after a real alteration and improvement of the situation. (1977, 817, cited by McBride, 2003, 142)

---

8 This is a topic which Thomas Merton, the Cistercian monk and prolific contemplative writer, felt passionately about. In seeking to escape from the contradictions and conflicts of his particular problematic world by entering a Cistercian monastery, Merton found he was confronted with another world which mirrored this – his interior one. Monica Furlong's (1980) biography of Merton offers an excellent overview of, and starting point from which to engage with Merton's perspectives.

As we mature as individuals, discovering in the company and with the aid of others more about our abilities, vulnerabilities and limitations, more about our embodied, sexual selves and our need for purposeful activity and play, we will not only deepen our understanding of self and enrich our relationships with others and God. We also may find ourselves more secure in the knowledge that as being beloved (warts and all) we belong; we have a role to play in enhancing the life of the world and the Coming of the Kingdom. In the complex pattern that is woven to form the tapestries of our local and global communities, we – each one of us – are an important, integral thread. To develop this understanding is at the core of finding meaning in our lives; precisely that which is at the heart of what we seek to help others do.

Bibliography

Ackermann, D. 1998. A Voice Was Heard in Ramah. In *Liberating Faith Practices*, edited by D. Ackermann and R. Bons-Storm, 75–102. Leuven: Peters.

Anderson, R. 2004. *Spiritual Caregiving as Secular Sacrament: A Practical Theology for Professional Caregivers*. London: Jessica Kingsley.

Antony, D., Decker, B. and Wilber, K. 1987. *Spiritual Choices*. New York: Paragon.

Astley, N. 2002 Introduction. In *Staying Alive: Real Poems for Unreal Times*, edited by N. Astley, 19–27. Tarset, Northumberland: Bloodaxe.

Au, W. and Cannon, N. 1995. *Urgings of the Heart: A Spirituality of Integration*. Mahwah, New Jersey: Paulist Press.

Auden, W. H. 1965. Introduction. In *The Protestant Mystics*, edited by A. Freemantle, 3–37. New York: Mentor Books.

—— 1979a. *Song for St Cecelia's Day II*. In *Selected Poems*, edited by E. Menedelson. London: Faber and Faber Limited.

—— 1979b. *Collected Sorter Poems 1927–1957*, edited by E. Mendelson. London: Faber and Faber.

—— 1981. *As I Walked Out One Evening*. In *The Rattle Bag*, edited by S. Heaney and T. Hughes, London: Faber and Faber Ltd.

Bailey, R. 1997. *Scarlet Ribbons: A Priest with Aids*. London: Serpent's Tail.

Ballard, P. 2008. Theological Reflection and Providence. *Practical Theology* 1(3): 285–9.

Barnes, M. C. 2009. *The Pastor as Minor Poet: Texts and Subtexts in the Ministerial Life*. Grand Rapids, MI.: Eerdman Publishing Company.

Bell, J. and Maule, G. 2005. Christ's Is the World in Which We Move. In *Church Hymnary* (4th edn). Norwich: Canterbury Press.

Bennett Moore, Z. 2002. *Introducing Feminist Perspectives on Pastoral Theology*. London: Sheffield Academic Press Ltd.

Berger, J. 1972. *Ways of Seeing*. London: Penguin Books Ltd.

Bergman, N. 2005. More Than a Cuddle: Skin-to-Skin Contact Is Key. *The Practising Midwife* 8(9): 44.

Bernanos, G. 1977. *The Diary of a Country Priest*. Translated by P. Morris. Glasgow: Collins, Fount Paperbacks.

Bibliography

Bettelheim, B. 1984. Afterward to C. Vegh, *I Didn't Say Goodbye* (R. Schwartz, Trans.). New York: E. P. Dutton.

Bolton, G. 2005. *Reflective Practice: Writing and Professional Development* (2nd edition). London: Sage.

Booty, J. (ed.) 1976. *The Book of Common Prayer 1559*. Charlottesville: University Press of Virginia.

Boyd. W. 2003. *Any Human Heart*. London: Penguin Books.

Browning Hesel, P. 2008. *In Memorium*: The Disenfranchised Grief of Chaplains and the Recovery of Memory. *The Journal of Pastoral Care and Counseling* 62(4): 337–42.

—— 2009. Liminality in Death Care: The Grief-Work of Pastors. *Journal of Pastoral Care and Counselling* 63(3,4): 1–7.

Brueggemann, W. 1984. *The Message of the Psalms: A Theological Commentary*. Minneapolis: Augsburg Publishing House.

Bugental, J. 1981. *The Search for Authenticity* (revised edition) New York: Irvington.

Burgess, R. 1999. Risk-Taking. In *Wrestling and Resting: Exploring Stories of Spirituality from Britain and Ireland*, edited by R. Harvey. London: Churches Together in Britain and Ireland.

Burnside, J. 2006. *Selected Poems*. London: Cape Poetry.

Cameron, H., Pallant, E. and Watchorn, H. 2005. Professional Identity, Regulation and Formation. *Contact* 145: 33–41.

Campbell, A. 1984. *Moderated Love: A Theology of Professional Care*. London: SPCK.

—— 1986. *Rediscovering Pastoral Care* (2nd edn). London: DLT.

Capps, D. 1993. *The Poet's Gift: Toward the Renewal of Pastoral Care*. Louisville, Kentucky: Westminster/John Knox Press.

—— 2005. *A Time to Laugh: The Religion of Humour*. New York: Continuum.

Carr, W. 2008. *The Pastor as Theologian: The Formation of Today's Ministry in the Light of Contemporary Human Sciences* (2nd edn). London: SPCK.

Carroll, M. 2009. From Mindless to Mindful Practice: on Learning Reflection in Supervision. *Psychotherapy in Australia* 15(4): 40–51.

Carter, A. and West, M. 1999. Sharing the Burden: Teamwork in Healthcare Settings. In *Stress in Health Professionals*, edited by J. Firth-Cozens and R. Payne, 191–202. Chichester: Wiley.

Carter, S. 2000. *The Two-Way Clock: Poems*. London: Stainer and Bell Ltd.

Carver, R. 1996. *All of Us: The Collected Poems*. London. The Harvill Press

Clark, D. 2002. Between Hope and Acceptance: The Medicalisation of Dying. *British Medical Journal* 324: 905–7.

Clark, T. 2009. *The Hundred Thousand Places*. Manchester: Carcanet Press.

Coe, J. 2008. *The Rotters' Club*. London: Penguin Books Ltd.

Cohen, L. 1992. Anthem. From *The Future*. Sony Music Entertainment Inc.

Bibliography

Cooper-White, P. 2006. Shared Wisdom: Use of the Self in Pastoral Care and Counseling (Person, Culture and Religion Group, American Academy of Religion, November 18, 2005). *Pastoral Psychology* 55: 233–41.

Cotter, J. (ed.) 1993. *Gather the Fragments: A Book of Days* (compiled by A. Ecclestone). Sheffield: Cairns Publications.

Couture, P. 1998. Feminist, Wesleyan, Practical Theology and the Practice of Pastoral Care. In *Liberating Faith Practices*, edited by D. Ackermann and R. Bons-Storm, 27–74. Leuven: Peters.

Danieli, Y. 2006. A Group Intervention to Process and Examine Countertransference near the End of Life. In *When Professionals Weep: Emotional and Countertransference Responses in End-of-Life Care*, edited by R. Katz and T. Johnson, 255–66. New York: Routledge.

Davidson, R. 1983. *The Courage to Doubt: Exploring an Old Testament Theme*. London: SCM Press.

Department of Health. 2010. *Robert Francis Inquiry Report into Mid-Staffordshire NHS Foundation Trust*. London: The Stationery Office.

Dostoevsky, F. 1949. *The Brothers Karamazov*. New York: Heritage Press.

Eadie, H. 1972. The Health of Scottish Clergymen. *Contact* 41 (Winter): 2–22.

Ellen, M. 2007. The Spin Doctor. *The Word* 53: 84–90.

Elliot, P. 2010. *Another World: Dali, Magritte, Miro and the Surrealists*. Edinburgh: National Galleries of Scotland.

Faludy, A, 2006. In Defence of Personhood: St Benedict and Postmodernity. *Contact* 151: 6–11.

Field, T. 2003. *Touch*. Massachusetts: Massachusetts Institute of Technology.

Firth-Cozens, J. and Cornwell, J. 2009. *The Point of Care: Enabling Compassionate Care in Acute Hospital Settings*. London: The King's Fund.

Fisher, J. and Gallant, S. 1990. Effect of Touch on Hospitalized Patients. In *Advances in Touch*, edited by N. Gunzenhauser, T. Brazelton and T. Field, 141–47. Skillman, NJ: Johnson & Johnson.

Fisher, J., Rytting, M. and Heslin, R. 1976. Affective and Evaluative Effects of an Interpersonal Touch. *Sociometry* 39: 416–21.

Fordham, F. 1966. *An Introduction to Jung's Psychology* (3rd edn). London: Pelican.

Forrester, D. 1997. *The True Church and Morality: Reflections on Ecclesiology and Ethics*. Geneva: WCC Publications.

Forrester, D., McDonald, I. and Tellini, G. 1996. *Encounter with God: An Introduction to Christian Worship and Practice* (2nd edn). London: Continuum.

Foskett, J. and Lyall, D. 1990. *Helping the Helpers: Supervision and Pastoral Care*. London: SPCK.

Fox, M. 1983. *Original Blessing*. Rochester, Vermont: Bear and Co.

Frost, R. 1981. Desert Places. In *The Rattle Bag*, edited by S. Heaney and T. Hughes. London: Faber and Faber Ltd.

Bibliography

Furlong, M. 1980. *Merton: A Biography.* London: SPCK.

Galloway, K. 1996. Desert 1. In *Talking to the Bones.* London: SPCK.

Gerkin, C. 1997. *An Introduction to Pastoral Care.* Nashville: Abingdon Press.

Ginsberg, A. 1999. Those Knowing Age. In *Death and Fame: Poems 1993–1997,* edited by R. Rosenthal, P. Hale and W. Morgan. London: Penguin Books.

Gomes, B. and Higginson, I. 2008. Where People Die (1974–2030): Past Trends, Future Projections and Implications for Care. *Palliative Medicine* 22: 33–41.

Graber, K. 2010. The Festival at Nikko. In *The Eternal City.* Princeton, NJ: Princeton University Press.

Graham, E. 2002. *Transforming Practice: Pastoral Theology in an Age of Uncertainty.* Eugene, OR: Wipf and Stock Publishers.

Green, R. 1987. *Only Connect.* London: DLT.

Greig, A. 1997. *Electric Brae.* Edinburgh: Cannongate.

—— 2006a. *Preferred Lies: A Journey to the Heart of Scottish Golf.* London: Weidenfield and Nicolson.

—— 2006b. *This Life: New and Selected Poems 1970–2006.* Tarset, Northumberland: Bloodaxe Books.

—— 2010. *At the Loch of the Green Corrie.* London: Quercus

Grenz, S. 1998. *Welcoming but Not Affirming.* Louisville: Westminster John Knox Press.

Grosch, W. and Olsen, D. 1994. *When Helping Starts to Hurt: A New Look at Burnout among Psychotherapists.* New York: Norton.

Harbaugh, G. 1984. *Pastor as Person: Maintaining Personal Integrity in the Choices and Challenges of Ministry.* Minneapolis, MN: Augsburg Publishing House.

Hare-Duke, M. 1994. *Hearing the Stranger.* Sheffield: Cairns Publications.

Hauerwas, S. 1990. *Naming the Silences.* Grand Rapids, MI: Eerdmans Publishing Co.

Hauerwas, S. and Wells, S. 2004. The Gift of the Church and the Gifts God Gives It. In *The Blackwell Companion to Christian Ethics,* edited by S. Hauerwas and S. Wells, 13–26. Oxford: Blackwell Publishing Ltd.

Henneally, C. 1997. *The New Curate.* Dublin: Mercier Press.

Herthe, K. 1990. Fostering Hope in Terminally-Ill People. *Journal of Advanced Nursing* 18: 1250–59.

Heyward, C. 1994. Notes on Historical Grounding: Beyond Sexual Essentialism. In *Sexuality and the Sacred: Sources for Theological Reflection,* edited by J. Nelson and S. Longfellow, 9–18. London: Mowbray.

Hill, D. 1987. *The New Century Bible Commentary: The Gospel of Matthew.* Grand Rapids, MI: Eerdmans Publishing Co.

Hinksman, B. 1999. Transference and Countertransference in Pastoral Counselling. In *Clinical Counselling in Pastoral Settings,* edited by G. Lynch. 94–106. London: Routledge.

House of Bishops of the General Synod of the Church of England. 2003. *Some Issues in Human Sexuality: A Guide to the Debate*. London: Church House Publishing.

Hunter, M. and Struve, J. 1998. *The Ethical Use of Touch in Psychotherapy*. London: Sage.

Hunter, R. 2005. Wisdom and Practical Knowledge. In *Dictionary of Pastoral Care and Counseling*, edited by R. Hunter, 1325–6. Nashville: Abingdon Press.

Irvine, A. 1997. *Between Two Worlds: Understanding and Managing Clergy Stress*. London: Mowbray.

Jacques, M. 2004. The Death of Intimacy. *The Guardian*, September 18.

Jansen, G. 2004. *Foundations of Violence: Death and the Displacement of Beauty*, Volume 1. London: Routledge.

Jones, G. and Armstrong, K. 2006. *Resurrecting Excellence: Shaping Faithful Christian Ministry*. Grand Rapids: Eerdmans.

Jourard, S. 1966. An Exploratory Study of Body Accessibility. *British Journal of Social and Clinical Psychology* 5: 221–31.

Jung, C. 1966. *The Practice of Psychotherapy*, vol. 16 of the Collected *Works of C. G. Jung*, trans. R. Hull. Princeton: Princeton University Press.

Jung, C. 1977. Depth Psychology and Self-Knowledge. In *The Collected Works of C. G. Jung*, edited by H. Read et al. London: Routledge and Kegan Paul.

Kaplinski, J. 2002. Death Does Not Come from Outside. In *Staying Alive: Real Poems for Unreal Times*, edited by N. Astley. Tarset, Northumberland: Bloodaxe Books.

Kay, J. 2010. *Red Dust Road*. London: Picador.

Kellaway, K. 2010. A Domestic Goddess Lost in Her Dreams. *The Observer: The New Review* 24 October, 43.

Kelly, E. 2007. *Marking Short Lives: Constructing and Sharing Rituals Following Pregnancy Loss*. Oxford: Peter Lang.

—— 2008. *Meaningful Funerals: Meeting the Theological and Pastoral Challenges in a Postmodern Era*. London: Mowbray.

Kenneally, C. 1997. *The New Curate*. Dublin: Mercier Press.

Kohut, H. 1971. *The Analysis of the Self: A Systematic Approach to the Psychoanalytic Treatment of Narcissistic Personality Disorders*. New York: International Universities Press.

Kornfield, M. 1998. *Cultivating Wholeness: A Guide to Care and Counseling in Faith Communities*. New York: Continuum.

Kramp, J. 2007. The Suicide of Thomas Merton. *Pastoral Psychology* 55: 619–35.

Kunitz, S. 1995. *Passing Through: The Later Poems, New and Selected*. New York: Norton.

LaCugna, C. 1991. *God for Us: The Trinity and the Christian Life*. San Francisco: Harper.

Bibliography

LaMothe, R. 2005. A Challenge to Church Leaders: The Necessity of Supervision for Ordained Ministers. *The Journal of Pastoral Care and Counseling* 59(1–2): 3–16.

Lawbaugh, W. 2005. Existential, Theological, and Psychological Concepts of Death: A Personal Retrospective. *The Journal of Pastoral Care and Counseling* 59(1–2): 17–27.

Leach, J. 2007. Pastoral Theology as Attention. *Contact: Practical Theology and Pastoral Care*. 153: 19–32

Leach, J. and Paterson, M. 2010. *Pastoral Supervision: A Handbook*. London: SCM Press.

Lewin, A. 2009. *Watching for the Kingfisher: Poems and Prayers*. Norwich: Poems and Prayers.

Litchfield, K. 2006. *Tend My Flock: Sustaining Good Pastoral Care*. Norwich: Canterbury Press.

Lyall, D. 2001. *Integrity of Pastoral Care*. London: SPCK.

Lyall, M. 1997. The Pastoral Counselling Relationship: A Touching Place? *Contact Pastoral Monograph* 7. Edinburgh: Contact Pastoral Trust.

MacCaig, N. 2009. A Corner of the Road, Early Morning. In *The Poems of Norman MacCaig*, edited by E. McCaig. Edinburgh: Polygon.

MacDiarmid, H. 1935. In the Slums of Glasgow. In *Hugh MacDiarmid: Selected Poetry*, edited by A.Riach and M. Grieve. 2004. Manchester: Carcanet Press Limited.

MacIntyre, A. 1987. *After Virtue: A Study in Moral Theology* (2nd edn). London: Duckworth.

MacKinlay, E. 2004. The Spiritual Dimension of Ageing. In *Ageing, Spirituality and Well-being*, edited by A. Jewell, 72–85. London: Jessica Kingsley.

MacMurray, J. 1961. *Persons in Relation*. London: Faber and Faber.

Malone, M. 2006. In the Raw. In *Running Threads*, poems by J. Hughes, R. Love, M. Malone and S Templeton. Troon: Makar Press.

McBride, D. 2003. *Waiting on God*. Chawton, Hampshire: Redemptorist Publications.

McGough, R. 2006. *Selected Poems*. London: Penguin Books.

Means, J. 2002. Mighty Prophet/Wounded Healer. *The Journal of Pastoral Care and Counselling* 56(1): 41–4.

Merton, T. 1972. *Seeds of Contemplation*. Wheathampstead: Anthony Clark.

Monbourquette, J. 2001. *How to Befriend your Shadow: Welcoming your Unloved Side*. Ottawa: Novalis, St Paul University.

Monroe, B. and Oliviere, D. 2006. Resilience in Palliative Care. *European Journal of Palliative Care* 13(1): 22–5.

Moore, B. 1997. *Black Robe*. New York: Plume.

Morrison, B. 2010. *The Last Weekend*. London: Chatto and Windus.

Mosse, B. 2003. *The Treasures of Darkness: A Spiritual Companion for Life's Watching and Waiting Times*. Norwich: Canterbury Press.

Bibliography

Muse, S. 2000. Keeping the Wellsprings of Ministry Clear. *The Journal of Pastoral Care* 54(3): 253–62.

Nelson, J. 1978. *Embodiment: An Approach to Sexuality and Christian Theology.* Minneapolis, MI: Augsburg Publishing House.

Newell, C. 2008. Better Dead Than Disabled? When Ethics and Disability Meet: A Narrative of Ageing, Loss and Exclusion. In *Ageing, Disability and Spirituality: Addressing the Challenge of Disability in Later Life,* edited by E. MacKinlay, 58–71. London: Jessica Kingsley Publications.

Newell, P. 2000. *Echo of the Soul: The Sacredness of the Human Body.* Norwich: Canterbury Press.

NHS Education for Scotland 2009. *Spiritual Care Matters: An Introductory Resource for all NHSScotland Staff.* Edinburgh: NHS Education for Scotland.

Nouwen, H. 1977. *The Living Reminder.* New York: Seabury Press.

—— 1978. *Creative Ministry.* New York: Image Books, Doubleday.

—— 1979. *The Wounded Healer.* New York: Image Books, Doubleday.

—— 1996. *Bread for the Journey.* London: DLT.

Owen, D. 2008. The 'Ah-Ha' Moment: Passionate Supervision as a Tool for Transformation and Metamorphosis. In *Passionate Supervision,* edited by R. Shohet, 50–68. London: Jessica Kingsley Publications.

Palmer, P. 1998. *The Courage to Teach: Exploring the Inner Landscape of a Teacher's Life.* San Fransisco: CA: Jossey-Bass.

Patton, J. 2005. *Pastoral Care: An Essential Guide.* Nashville: Abingdon Press.

Patton, J. F. 2006. Jungian Spirituality: A Developmental Context for Late-life Growth. *American Journal of Hospice and Palliative Medicine* 23(4): 304–8.

Paulson, D. 2006. The Search for Spiritual Integrity. *Pastoral Psychology* 55: 197–204.

Pembroke, N. 2006. *Renewing Pastoral Practice.* Aldershot: Ashgate.

—— 2007. *Moving Toward Spiritual Maturity: Psychological and Moral Challenges in Christian Living.* New York: Haworth Pastoral Press.

Pines, A. and Aronson, E. 1988. *Burnout: Causes and Cures* (2nd edn) New York: free Press.

Pohly, K. 1993. *Transforming the Rough Places: The Ministry of Supervision.* Dayton, OH: Whaleprints.

Ramsay, N. 2004. Contemporary Pastoral Theology: A Wider Vision for the Practice of Love. In *Pastoral Care and Counseling: Redefining the Paradigms,* edited by N. Ramsay, 155–176. Nashville, TN: Abingdon Press.

Remen, R. 2006. *Kitchen Table Wisdom, Stories that Heal* (10th Anniversary Edition). New York: Riverhead Books.

Roberts, M. 2007. Threads in the Formation of Faithful Clergy. *Contact* 152: 31–39.

Robinson, M. 2005. *Gilead.* London: Virago Press.

Robinson, S. 2008. *Spirituality, Ethics and Care.* London: Jessica Kingsley.

Rose, S. 2008. Eighth Day. In *Poems in the Waiting Room.* Autumn 2008

Bibliography

Rudd, A. 2010. Dwelling. *Living Spirituality News* Spring: 3.

Ryan, S. 2008. Mindful Supervision. In *Passionate Supervision*, edited by R. Shohet, 70–85. London: Jessica Kingsley Publishers.

Sandford, J. 1992. *Ministry Burnout*. Lousville, KY. Presbyterian Publishing Corporation.

Schaufeli, W. 1999. Burnout. In *Stress in Healthcare Professionals*, edited by J. Firth-Cozens and R.Payne, 17–32. Chichester: Wiley.

Scott, K. 2005. In the Nature of Things. *The Guardian Review* 18 June: 20–3.

Sellner, E. 1990. *Mentoring: The Ministry of Spiritual Kinship*. Notre Dame, IN: Ave Marie Press.

Seymour, J., French, J. and Richardson, E. 2010. Dying Matters: Let's Talk about it. *British Medical Journal* 341: 646–8.

Shakespeare, W. 1981. Aye, but to die, and go we know not where. In *The Rattle Bag*, edited by S. Heaney and T. Hughes. London: Faber and Faber Ltd.

Shannon, W. 1985. *The Hidden Ground of Love: The Letters of Thomas Merton and Religious Experience and Social Concerns*. New York, NY: Farrar, Straus and Giroux.

Sims, N. 2008. Power and Supervision in the Context of the Church and its Ministry. *Practical Theology* 1(2): 203–17.

Smith, H. and Smith, M. 2008. *The Art of Helping Others: Being Around, Being There, Being Wise*. London: Jessica Kingsley Publishers.

Smith, R. 1990. *Living in Covenant with God and One Another: A Guide to the Study of Sexuality and Human Relations using Statements from Member Churches of the World Council of Churches*. Geneva: World Council of Churches.

Sontag, S. 2006. To Stand Still Is to Fall away from the Truth. *The Guardian G2*, 14 September: 7-11.

Spence, A. 1998. *Way to Go*. London: Phoenix House.

Stairs, J. 2000. *Listening for the Soul: Pastoral Care and Spiritual Direction*. Minneapolis: Fortress Press.

Stafford, W. 1977. *Stories That Could Be True: New and Collected Poems*. New York: Harper and Row.

Stewart, M. 1997. Insides and Outsides: Sexuality as Life Journey. In *Dreaming of Eden: Reflections on Christianity and Sexuality*, edited by K. Galloway, 17–26. Glasgow: Wild Goose Publications.

Streets, F. 1996. Bearing the Spirit Home. In *Facing Death: Where Culture, Religion and Medicine Meet*, edited by H. Spiro, M. McCrea Curnen and L. Palmer Wandel, 180–83. New Haven: Yale University Press.

Sutherland, M. 2006. *The Science of Parenting*. London: Dorling Kindersley.

Swinton, J. 2007. *Raging with Compassion: Pastoral Responses to the Problem of Evil*. Grand Rapids, MI: Eerdmans Publishing Co.

Taylor, E. 2007. *What Do I Say: Talking to Patients about Spirituality*. Philadelphia: Templeton Foundation Press.

Bibliography

Thomas. R. S. 1986. *Selected Poems 1946–1968*. Newcastle upon Tyne: Bloodaxe Books, Ltd.

—— 1993. *Collected Poems 1945–1990*. London: Phoenix Giants.

Ulanov, A. and Dueck, A. 2008. *The Living God and Our Living Psyche: What Christians Can Learn from Carl Jung*. Grand Rapids, MI: Eerdmans.

Uphoff, A. 2008. Touch and the Therapeutic Relationship: Shifting a Paradigm. In *The Therapeutic Relationship: Perspectives and Themes*, edited by S. Haugh and S. Paul, 203–15. Ross-on-Wye: PCCS Books Ltd.

Vanistendael, S. 2003. *Resilience and Spirtituality*. Geneva: BICE (unpublished paper).

Vanstone, W. H. 1982. *The Statue of Waiting*. London: DLT.

Ward, F. 2005. *Lifelong Learning: Theological Education and Supervision*. London: SCM Press.

Webster, A. 2002. *Wellbeing*. London: SCM Press.

Wells, S. 2007. *Power and Passion: Six Characters in Search of Resurrection*. Grand Rapids, MI: Zondervan.

Wells, S. and Quash, B. 2010. *Introducing Christian Ethics*. Chichester: Wiley-Blackwell.

Wilber, K. 1982. *The Spectrum of Consciousness*. Wheaton, IL: Theosophical Publishing House.

White, V. 2002. *Identity*. London: SCM Press.

Williams, R. 2002a. *Poems of Rowan Williams*. Oxford: The Perpetua Press.

—— 2002b. *The Body's Grace* (2nd edn). London: Lesbian and Gay Christian Movement and The Institute for the Study of Christianity and Sexuality.

—— 2007. Foreward. In *Power and Passion: Six Characters in Search of Resurrection* by S. Wells, 9–10. Grand Rapids, MI: Zondervan.

Willows, D. and Swinton, J. 2000. Introduction. In *Spiritual Dimensions of Pastoral Care*, edited by D. Willows and J. Swinton, 11–16. London: Jessica Kingsley.

Woodward, J. 2005. *Befriending Death*. London: SPCK.

Wren, B. 2005. Great God Your Love Has Called Us Here. In *Church Hymnary* (4th edn). Norwich: Canterbury Press.

Yalom, I. 2008. *Staring at the Sun: Overcoming the Dread of Dead*. London: Piatkus.

All quotations from the Holy Bible are taken from the *New Revised Standard Version* 1989 Peabody, MA: Hendrickson Publishers, unless otherwise stated.

Index

Index

191